PHOTOSHOP CS2 FOR ADVERTISING AND MARKETING

Secrets from an Entertainment Advertising Insider

DANIEL O. SORENSON

Peachpit
Press

Photoshop CS2 for Advertising and Marketing:
Secrets from an Entertainment Advertising Insider

Daniel O. Sorenson

Peachpit Press
1249 Eighth Street
Berkeley, CA 94710
510/524-2178
510/524-2221 (fax)

Find us on the Web at www.peachpit.com

To report errors, please send a note to errata@peachpit.com

Peachpit Press is a division of Pearson Education

Development Editor: Richard Theriault
Project Editor: Suzie Nasol
Production Editor: Hilal Sala
Technical Editor: Victor Gavenda
Compositor: Kim Scott
Indexer: Rebecca Plunkett
Cover design: Mimi Heft, Ellen Reilly
Cover illustration: Daniel O. Sorenson
Interior design: Kim Scott

ISBN 0-321- 35028-6

9 8 7 6 5 4 3 2 1

Printed and bound in the United States of America

To my wife Aya and son Kan,
who have brought joy and meaning to my life.

ACKNOWLEDGEMENTS

No book is born without the extraordinary effort of many people. I would like to thank the following persons for making this book possible.

Marjorie Baer, Executive Acquisitions Editor
for believing in me and my vision.

Victor Gavenda, Senior Technical Editor
for making sure what I tell you is correct, and making it seem that I know what I am talking about.

Richard Theriault, Senior Editor
for making the process fun, championing the concept and purpose of the book, and keeping it true to the original vision. And for his persnickety editing (he'd say meticulous, but persnickety fits) that forced me to consider every detail no matter how small and resulted in a better end product.

Suzie Nasol, Project Editor/Manager
for keeping things on track, making quick executive decisions, and quickly responding to every concern I had.

Kim Scott, Designer/Compositor
for pulling together an extraordinary design.

Mimi Heft and Ellen Reilly, Cover Designers
for bringing our dynamic cover to life.

Hilal Sala, Production Editor
for juggling all the pieces and ensuring they got to the printer on time.

Val Gelineau, CEO PhotoSpin.com
for providing my readers and me with all of the great images in this book and on the CD.

Katrin Eismann, one of my first Photoshop instructors, who introduced me to the magic of Photoshop, and helped me get this book off the ground.

Neil Salkind of Studio B, my agent, who looked out for my interest, helped me understand the process, and gave me endless encouragement when times got rough.

I owe a debt to all my students at UCLA and Otis College of Art and Design. They helped me discover my love of teaching, and in the end, they taught me far more than I taught them. I would especially like to thank Dorine Moreno, who convinced me I had something of value to offer and encouraged me to write a book; and students of my summer Otis class who worked through the book in its rough form and helped iron out the kinks: Lisa Castle, Renee Clark, Toni Dicks, and Franklin Fodel.

Thank you to those friends and associates whose support and encouragement went beyond the call of duty, in particular Andy Aryapour, Bill Wilson, and Tony Robbins.

contents

ANIME ILLUSTRATION, 2

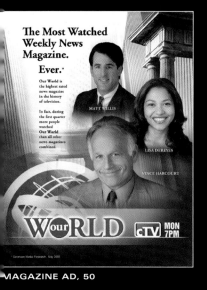

MAGAZINE AD, 50

MUSIC PROMO, 96

OUTDOOR AD CAMPAIGN, 130

MOVIE POSTER, 164

intro

CTION INTRODUCTION INTRODUCTION INTRODUCTION INTRODUCTION INTRODUCTION INT

duction

Listen up!

This book is the product of what I have learned over the last

15 years working as a designer and art director in the enter-

tainment industry and also through my experience teach-

ing Adobe Photoshop at UCLA and Otis College of Art and

Design. The projects you'll be creating all relate specifically

to the entertainment industry—but the graphic design prin-

ciples and Photoshop techniques that you will learn apply

to virtually any area of advertising and marketing.

In putting this book together, I have tried to create the book that I wish I'd had when I was first starting out with Photoshop and digital imaging. It is more than a project-based book to teach essential Photoshop skills to aspiring graphic designers and digital artists. It's also a design book and a marketer's primer, with an industry insider's unique look at life in the demanding, high-speed world of entertainment marketing. Yes, you will learn to do amazing things with images in a very short period of time, but you will learn more than that. You'll learn that good advertising is more than simply dispensing information. Good advertising uses color, typography, lighting effects, and storytelling techniques as tools for creating an emotional response in the viewer, motivating him or her to take action. When you understand how to apply each of these principles—and how to harness the power of Photoshop to let you work creatively, spontaneously, and nondestructively—you can create marketing campaigns that are sexy, funny, suspenseful, mysterious, and, most of all, compelling, whatever the product (or client) calls for. This is the stuff of entertainment. It is the stuff of all great advertising. If that is the business you want to be in, this book is for you.

HOW THIS BOOK WORKS

The book is organized to benefit anyone at least basically familiar with Photoshop as well as designers who have substantial Photoshop experience.

Structure and purpose

The instruction in this book is structured around five entertainment-oriented projects: an Anime illustration, a magazine ad, key art for music promo, a billboard for an outdoor campaign, and a movie poster. Try not to rush through the projects. The point isn't to exactly reproduce my finished version of the project, but to *understand* what you are doing so you can apply it to a different situation. This isn't about finishing as fast as you can. It's about really understanding how Photoshop thinks so you can use it in the real world.

Mini-Tutorials

From time to time as you work through a project, you'll see a reference to a Mini-Tutorial, a hands-on practice lesson at the end of the project that goes into depth on a particular tool or technique. If you are confident in your knowledge of that tool or technique, feel free to move on with the project. If you are unfamiliar with or feel a bit rusty with that tool and could use a little refresher on it, take a short break to work through the lesson. These mini-tutorials are there to insure that you have a good foundation in the basics. Don't shortchange yourself by skipping them.

Photoshop Essentials

Occasionally the text will call your attention to a Photoshop Essential, also placed at the end of the project. These are topics directly related to Photoshop that are "must knows" for anyone working in commercial graphics. It's best not to proceed until you are *sure* you understand them.

As the book progresses the projects become more difficult. Each builds on what was learned in the previous projects, so skills and techniques are honed and perfected. Newer users will do well to work from start to finish, and experienced users may want to hop around, tackling the project they find most interesting. Begin with any project you like, depending on your current skill level. Just don't cheat yourself by jumping to the more difficult projects before you've thoroughly reviewed the less difficult ones. This can't be stressed enough: There's no substitute for a good foundation in the basics.

Tools and images

Over the years, Photoshop has gained many tools from version to version. This book will cover only those tools and techniques that I feel are currently relevant and that I actually use on the job. We won't spend time on tools that I haven't found useful or that are what I call destructive. One very useful feature is keyboard shortcuts—there is a keyboard shortcut for almost everything you wish to do. A list of my favorites is provided in the Appendix and I

WORKING NONDESTRUCTIVELY—AND STAYING ALIVE

This may be the most important concept in the book, and its importance cannot be overstated. By working nondestructively, I mean working in a way that allows you to make changes quickly. It's a way of working that keeps as many options open as possible. Because in the world of entertainment changes happen—and they happen most often when you're out of time with everyone breathing down your neck.

Here's what I mean. A couple of years ago I was preparing a series of Emmy consideration ads for *The Hollywood Reporter* and *Daily Variety*. I had been working on the ads for weeks. They had already gone through multiple changes during the approval process. They were due at those two publications the next morning by 10. The creative team had already been given a deadline extension and there was no more wiggle room. The files had to be delivered to the prepress house by 8 that night in order for them to guarantee delivery to the pubs by 10 the next morning. So here it was, 5 p.m., a messenger was standing by, and the ads were just being shown for the first time to the president of the network. By 5:30 the president, the vice president of public relations and his assistant, the vice president of marketing, and my design director were standing behind me while I was frantically making changes to

the ads. In the meantime the prepress house called several times asking when the files would be delivered and the publications called saying that if the ads were not to them by 10 a.m. they were going to run blank pages. That meant the network would be paying nearly $50,000 for blank pages! The problem was that the president didn't feel the ads captured the true spirit of the shows. He wanted major changes. Four ads had to be changed…immediately.

I think you get the picture. Unfortunately, this scenario is not at all unusual in the entertainment business. In fact, it's more often the rule than the exception. Everyone involved in the approval process brings to the table his or her own experience, agenda, strategy. As an ad campaign is developed and discussed, strategies change, budgets change, politics come into play. Too often the person with the final sign-off authority doesn't even see your work until it is almost too late to make the deadline. Inevitably he brings a different point of view. For you, that means changes.

Photoshop gives you the nondestructive tools to stay flexible to the end, make last-minute changes, and still possibly get home in time for dinner. ■

will refer to different ones frequently throughout the book. Whether you are using a Mac or Windows computer, the keyboard shortcuts are essentially the same except for the names of the modifier keys. Wherever a keyboard shortcut is mentioned, the keystrokes for both platforms will be shown. The Mac shortcut will be followed by a slash and then the Windows shortcut—for example Command-N/Ctrl-N (the Mac/Win keyboard shortcuts for creating a new document).

The appendix also contains lists of all tools and techniques covered throughout the book, first grouped by the project that included them, then listed alphabetically. It's a good place to look for reminders or refresher brush-ups.

All the images for the projects and mini-tutorials are provided on the accompanying CD. I suggest you copy all of these to a folder on your hard drive then put the CD away for safekeeping.

All photographic images for the projects and tutorials have been provided by PhotoSpin.com. You may download the images for educational purposes only. They may not be used in products or projects for commercial use or resale. PhotoSpin Assets of any resolution cannot be resold, whether individually, in collections, or modified.

WRAPPING IT UP

Working nondestructively is the guiding principle of this book. The sidebar has told you why; throughout the book I'll show you how. This is a new way of working for most of you, so there will be reminders from time to time to help you get in the habit. Professionally, it will save your life.

Enjoy your journey and build your skills. When you have finished all the projects and mastered all the tools and techniques in this book, you will be well prepared to start working in marketing and advertising.

illustration

ANIME ILLUSTRATION

EVERY ILLUSTRATION, PHOTOGRAPHIC IMAGE, OR
graphic design is more successful if it tells a story and
evokes an emotion. Whenever you start a job, ask yourself
what is the story I am telling, and *to whom I am telling it?*
The answers to these two questions will inform important
decisions you make all along the way.

In this project, you will work with black-and-white line art,
adding color and the illusion of three dimensions, to create an illustration aimed at young males 8 to 12 years old.
This is an age group that often feels powerless and has a
strong desire to be recognized as being significant. That's
why animations and video games featuring superheroes

1

overcoming danger and defeating powerful enemies are so popular among boys this age. There—I've just defined the audience and outlined the main elements of the story. Our hero, Zaan, is coming from a place of power and energy, light and warmth. He is entering a darker, cooler, mysterious place where he will surely confront danger. He is not afraid. His attitude is confident, even defiant. There is no doubt about who will win this conflict.

Colors that appeal to this age group, though more sophisticated than the primary colors that appeal to smaller children, are still usually highly saturated. Rather than just red, blue, and green, you may find burgundy, aqua blues, hot pink, verillian, green, and many variations of purple. Often these colors will be juxtaposed with their opposites (complements) on the color wheel for a complex and interesting visual experience. Contrast is an important element in all imagery and design, and there are different types of contrast—light and dark, warm and cool, large and small, simple and complex. Learn to see them. Then, learn to use them.

The project is divided into three parts. First you will set up the document and fill the main areas with solid flat colors. The second part will introduce you to the art of creating three-dimensional illustration. Using the Brush and Gradient tools and Layer clipping masks you will quickly and painlessly add dimension and richness to your illustration. Finally, you'll create a dynamic background that will complete your illustration, giving your hero an environment in which to exist and carry out his amazing feats.

Here are some of the Photoshop tools and techniques you will learn about in this project:

✔ Layers and layer groups

✔ Magic Wand tool

✔ Color Picker

✔ Layer clipping masks

✔ Airbrush

✔ Gradient tool and Gradient Editor

✔ Blur filter

✔ Layer blend modes

Start by opening the document **Anime.psd** located in the Project One folder on the CD (**FIGURE 1-1**).

FIGURE 1-1

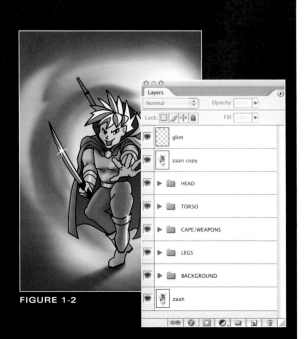

FIGURE 1-2

Set up the document and fill the main areas with color

Layers are one of Photoshop's most valuable features for working nondestructively. Layers allow you to separate the various elements of the image so you can easily modify them individually later. In this project, every area of our hero's body and clothing is going to be colored on a separate layer. Take a look at the completed illustration for a moment and you'll realize this can mean a lot of layers, tons of them (**FIGURE 1-2**). People who are new to Photoshop are often reluctant to use a lot of layers, thinking that working this way is less efficient, or something. Get over it. When you're working nondestructively, more is more. Photoshop supports virtually unlimited layers, so don't worry about running out. The only drawback to having lots of layers is that you quickly increase the file size. Hard drives and storage space are cheap and plentiful these days, but you also want to make sure you have enough RAM—lots of it—and, ideally, a fast computer.

Photoshop is on the leading edge of technology, and its demands, as well as the computers available to run it, are moving targets. The basic needs will be different depending on whether you're creating images for print, on-air, or the Web, so there's no single "minimum formula." The best recommendation is to install as much RAM as your computer will allow. Photoshop will run on almost any computer and there's no absolute minimum processor requirement, but you'll spend less time waiting and make more money with the fastest computer you can afford and the latest system software.

The goal of this project is to give you a solid understanding of layers and the Layers palette, and how to organize a Photoshop document. First you will render the illustration of Zaan, our anime hero. Then, you will create the background. The order in which you do things in this project isn't necessarily the order in which you would do them if this were a real job. In a real job situation, you might want to start with the background to establish the color palette and light source first or your client might want to see several color schemes for the clothing before you even begin to think about the background and light sources. Each job is different. In future projects you will work in a more fluid way, moving between background and foreground layers as the composite develops.

Before you begin building your document, you should have a basic understanding of layers and the Layers palette. **Photoshop Essential 1.1** (at the end of this project) explains the origin of the Layers palette metaphor and gives you an overview of how it works and many of the features found there.

SET UP LAYERS

Having lots of layers is a good thing, but navigating through them can be a bear. To make things easier and conserve valuable monitor real estate Photoshop gives us Layer groups (previously called Layer sets). Layer groups (just called *groups* hereafter) let you organize your layers into collections. To open or close a group click the little triangle next to the group icon in the Layers palette. When a group is open you can see all the layers inside; close it and they are all hidden.

Start by creating a group for each major area of the illustration. Press the Option key (Mac)/Alt (Win) and click the *create new group* button at the bottom of the Layers palette. This will bring up the New Group dialog (**FIGURE 1-3**). Name the group **LEGS** and click OK. If you simply click the *create new group* button without pressing the Option/Alt key a new unnamed group will automatically be added to the Layers palette. To name it, click the word *Group*, then type the new name. Make a habit of naming your groups and layers—this will help you navigate through the Layers palette later. I divided the illustration into four groups: HEAD, TORSO, CAPE/ WEAPONS, LEGS (**FIGURE 1-4**). I suggest naming groups with a format that distinguishes them from layers. An easy way to do this is to use all uppercase for groups and all lowercase for layers.

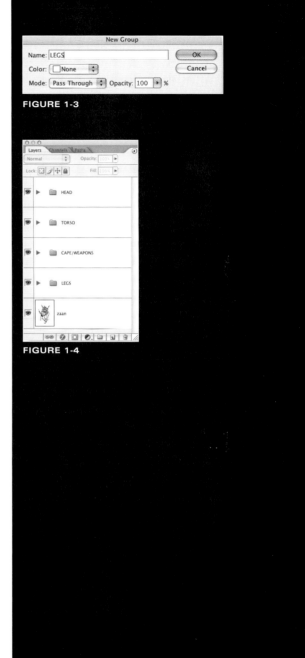

FIGURE 1-3

FIGURE 1-4

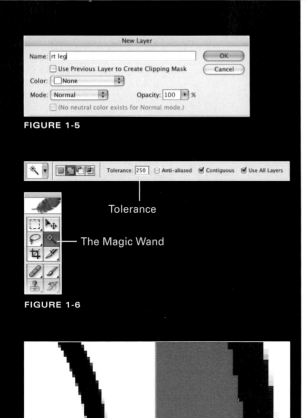

FIGURE 1-5

Tolerance

The Magic Wand

FIGURE 1-6

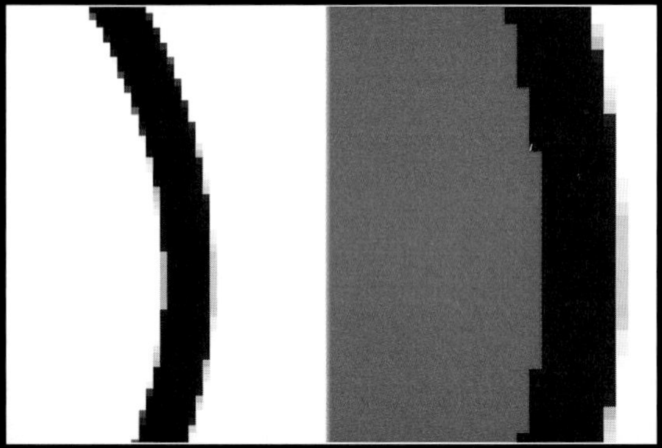

FIGURE 1-7

CREATE LAYERS, SELECTIONS, AND COLOR FILLS

Whenever a group is highlighted and the little triangle just to the left of the group icon is pointing down, that group is open and any layer you create will automatically become a member of it.

1. Highlight and open the group LEGS. Now hold down Option/ Alt and click the *create new layer* button at the bottom of the palette. This will bring up the New Layer dialog (**FIGURE 1-5**). Name the layer *right leg*. (Remember, we're using all lower-case for layer names to distinguish them from group names.)

Now, you will make a selection of the pants and fill the selection with color.

2. Click the Magic Wand tool (**FIGURE 1-6**). Take a moment to look at the choices in the options bar at the top of your screen. The Magic Wand makes a selection based on a value or color range, determined by the Tolerance you specify.

    ➤ The default setting of 32 would be fine if this were truly a black-and-white image. But use the Zoom tool (Command-Spacebar/Ctrl-Spacebar) to "marquee" (click and drag) around a small portion of the line art to view it really up close and personal (**FIGURE 1-7**). Notice the line is not 100% black and it is not smooth. That's because I created this illustration in Adobe Illustrator, a vector application, then brought it into Photoshop, a raster application. The illustration became *rasterized*.

    ➤ It's important to understand the difference between vector-based art and raster-based art and the role of anti-aliasing. If these concepts are new to you, be sure to read **Photo-shop Essential 1.2** (at the end of this project).

WORK NONDESTRUCTIVELY AND PROTECT YOUR ASSETS

The concept and importance of working nondestructively was presented in the introduction. In this project you will learn the basic strategy of working nondestructively, something that will be stressed throughout this book. Basically, working nondestructively means working in a way that keeps your options open. Last minute changes are a fact of life in advertising and marketing. Working nondestructively will allow you to accommodate those changes with minimal stress and maximum effectiveness. When working nondestructively you never want to flatten your working document (merge layers or groups). Even if you choose to send a flattened version to the printer you will want to preserve the layered version in case you need to make changes at the last minute or revise the ad in the future.

Become fanatical about saving your document. It is easy to so engrossed in your work that you forget to do this. Then suddenly the unthinkable happens, your computer crashes and an hour's work is lost. If working on an original scan (as opposed to bringing the scan into a new document) first do a Save As (File > Save As). Name the document something different to distinguish it from the original. You might name it ProjectOne_V1 for example. Choose Photoshop from the format menu. Be sure the Layers box is checked. Click OK. This will preserve the original document in case you mess up and need to start over. From now on to save your document simply press Command-S/Ctrl-S. Do this often. ■

THE MAGIC WAND TOOL—HANDLE WITH CARE

Normally, I don't recommend using the Magic Wand tool. The Magic Wand is one of Photoshop's quick and easy, down and dirty tools. It determines what is to be selected based on values (relative darkness and lightness) or color. It's a favorite of beginners because it seems so easy. But don't become dependent on this tool. It is one of the least predictable of the lot. This is one of the rare situations where the Magic Wand works well because we are dealing with a high contrast line illustration. For most continuous tone images or illustrations with gradations, this is not the tool of choice. ■

3. What does this have to do with making selections using the Magic Wand? Look again at Figure 1-7. If you leave the tolerance at 32, any selection you make will stop at the medium gray pixels. For best results the selection should go right up to the black pixels. That means you need to increase the tolerance.

➤ Try a setting of 250—that should get your selection right up to the black. As you start filling in your selections with color, you may notice that the lines are getting thinner. That's because the gray areas of the anti-aliased edges are disappearing.

Tip: Near the end of this project I will show you a little trick to change that.

GROUPS AND LAYERS

I ended up with a total of 28 layers within four groups. Note that the layer *zaan* is not in a group because it is the background layer.

HEAD	TORSO	CAPE/WEAPONS	LEGS
face	chest	cape left side	left boot
dark hair	left arm	cape right side	left leg
light hair	left hand	cape inside	right boot
tongue	left arm band	sword left side	right leg
eyes/teeth	right arm	sword right side	
	right hand	left shinai (martial	zaan ■
	right arm band	arts weapon)	
	shirt/sleeves	right shinai	
	medallion		

➤ Be sure to choose Contiguous and Sample All Layers in the options bar. That will restrict your selection to areas defined by the black lines. Be sure to highlight the second selection option (Add to Selection) in the options bar. That way you can select several areas in succession, adding to the selection with each click. This will be useful when an element you want on one layer is divided by another element in the image.

4. With *right leg* highlighted, click within the outlined area of Zaan's pants. Voilà! The leg is selected. By the way, references to right and left are from the viewer's point of view. So "right leg" means the leg on your right, not Zaan's right.

➤ To choose a color for the pants, click the Foreground color in the toolbox. This brings up the Color Picker (**FIGURE 1-8**). In the default state of the color picker, color is defined by its hue, saturation, and brightness. Choose a hue from the vertical bar and click in the Color field to define the saturation and brightness. Choose a color that you like and click OK.

5. Go to Edit > Fill, choose Foreground Color from the *Use* menu, and click OK. The keyboard shortcut for filling a selection with the foreground color is Option-Delete/Alt-Backspace. After you have filled the selection, *BE SURE TO DESELECT* (Command-D/Ctrl-D). If you don't deselect, the next action you take will affect the selection you just filled.

Each element of the illustration should be on its own layer. Sometimes parts of one element are divided by other elements. The inside of the cape, for example, is divided into several pieces by Zaan's body. Selecting all the parts is slightly different from selecting the right leg.

1. Highlight and open the group CAPE/WEAPONS. Option/Alt-click the New Layer button to open the New Layer dialog. Name the new layer *cape inside*.

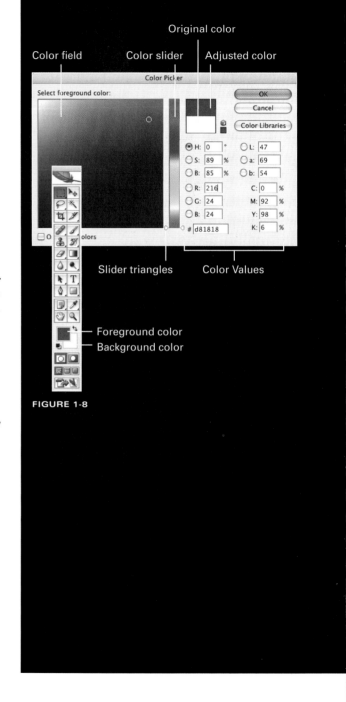

FIGURE 1-8

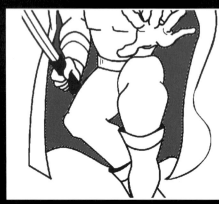

FIGURE 1-9

2. Since you chose the Add to Selection option, you can select the entire inside of the cape simply by clicking each of its areas. Each click will add to the selection.

3. As you did for the pants, choose a color for the inside of the cape and fill the selection. Again, don't forget to deselect after you have filled the area (**FIGURE 1-9**). It will be necessary to zoom in close to select small areas, the piece of the inside cape that is between the legs, for example. You can select and color the rest of the image using this technique, being sure to get all the little areas. The whites of the eyes and the teeth, for example are easy to miss. Be sure to fill them with white.

Tip: When you are working in close, it is helpful to use the Space-bar keystroke to access the hand tool. Click and drag to move to various areas of the image. You can quickly zoom in by pressing Command-Plus (+)/Ctrl-Plus (+) or zoom out by pressing Command-Minus (–)/Ctrl-Minus (–). To fit the image to the screen press Command-0 (zero)/Ctrl-0 (zero).

Each layer should be within the appropriate group. However, don't worry if you put one in the wrong group. You can drag it into the correct group at any time. The Groups and Layers sidebar is a list of the groups and layers I made for the project document. You can create yours all at once before you make any selections, or create them one at time as you make and fill selections.

You can use many tricks to create the illusion of 3D in your images. The sidebar *Creating Three-Dimensional Illustrations* introduces you to some of the basics of 3D along with some general tips about creating illustrations.

As you continue coloring your illustration, try to pick colors that will define the light source and enhance the sense of depth. For example the leg on the left is farther away from the viewer and is shaded by the body. It will be a little darker, cooler, and less satu-rated than the one on the right. The leg on the right is forward, closer to the viewer and is getting direct light along the right side. It will be warmer, brighter, more saturated. The Eyedropper will be a valuable tool here.

With the Eyedropper tool active, click an existing color in your image and that color becomes the foreground color. You can then click the Foreground color box to bring up the Color Picker and modify the color. Let's say you filled the leg on the right with a particular shade of red (**FIGURE 1-10**) then worked on something else. When it comes time to color the leg on the left, use the Eyedropper to sample the color of the right leg, click the Foreground color box to bring up the Color Picker, then pick a color that is slightly darker and cooler. This will give the illustration a more natural look.

Continue to use this select-and-fill method and color the entire image. When you have finished, it should look something like **FIGURE 1-11**.

Add dimension

Now to add some dimension to our hero. This is where Photoshop starts to be fun. You are going to learn about one of my favorite features, the Layer clipping mask. Masks allow you to make part of a layer or group invisible without erasing or deleting anything. They are totally nondestructive—you can easily modify or get rid of masks with no harm done. The Layer clipping mask works a little differently from other masks, by using use one layer to mask or *clip* another. The layer acting as the mask hides everything on the other layer except where the two overlap. It is as if you took a pair of scissors and "clipped" away the excess—except that in this case the excess is merely hidden, not eliminated. Used with the Brush and Gradient tools, Layer clipping masks make adding highlights and shadows a breeze.

The Brush and Gradient tools are so important and so powerful, Mini-Tutorials 1.1 and 1.2 at the end of the project deal specifically with these items. You will use both of these tools in every project from now on. Work these tutorials to make sure you have them nailed.

FIGURE 1-10

FIGURE 1-11

CREATING THREE-DIMENSIONAL ILLUSTRATIONS

We are all familiar with the principles of 3D—we just don't know we are. They allow us to function in the physical world. It's one thing to be familiar with them on a subconscious level, but another to understand them consciously and put them to proper use in our images. Many times otherwise good work falls apart because someone didn't pay attention to these simple principles. Using them correctly will help you move from amateur to professional.

FIGURE 1-12

The number one key to making an illustration look 3D is to have a consistent, clearly defined light source, a spot from which the light is emanating. Light and shadow give us the information we need to determine the volume and weight of an object (**FIGURE 1-12**). An object must have both of these to appear 3D. The way light hits an object and "falls off" or fades away tells us the shape and texture of the object. The shadow an object casts gives us an idea of how heavy it is and its location in space. An object resting on a plane, the ground for instance, will have a cast shadow that touches the object. If the object and shadow don't touch, the object will appear to be suspended or floating. The cast shadow will be darkest right at the point where the object and the plane meet. It will get lighter the farther away it is from the object because of reflected or ambient light. Everything in nature is affected by light either directly or indirectly. That's why you never see truly solid flat color in nature. Cast shadows are no exception. Even the darkest shadow is not 100% opaque. To get a better understanding of how light and shadow work you may find it helpful to study black-and-white photographs.

Detail and focus can help create a sense of depth. When a viewer with normal vision looks at a scene, objects closer to the viewer appear sharper and more detailed than those farther away. Areas in light have more detail than areas in shadow. Rembrandt was well aware of this and created an enormous sense of depth by putting great detail in the lighted areas of his pictures and almost none in the shadow areas. An object closer to the viewer has more contrast and colors are more saturated. Another factor that can affect depth is the temperature of colors. The closer a color approaches blue, the cooler it is said to be. The closer it approaches red, the warmer it is. Warmer colors tend to advance visually and cooler colors tend to recede. It's interesting to note that the temperature of the light source affects the temperature of the highlights and shadows in an image. Sunlight is warm. So, in an image lit by the sun, the light areas will lean toward the warm side of the spectrum and shadows toward the cool. In images lit by the moon, just the opposite is true. Artificial light can be either warm or cool depending on the type of light bulbs being used. Often an image will have a warm main light source, and cool secondary or reflected light source as in my final version of Project 1.

Perspective, of course, is another important aspect of 3D, far too complex to discuss in detail here. It's important to remember that Photoshop is not a 3D modeling program. It is a 2D program that, using the principles mentioned above, can create the *illusion* of 3D, and that illusion can be very believable. A client actually asked me to rotate a car in one of my images so it could be viewed more from the top. He was so accustomed to the 3D illusions I was creating in Photoshop that he really found it hard to believe I couldn't just change the camera angle. I had to explain that as realistic as the car looked, it was not a 3D model. In Photoshop we have very limited ability to change perspective or camera angle. If we try to do so, the object will become flattened out. One aspect of perspective we do have control over is scale. Things closer to the viewer appear larger. As they get farther away, they appear smaller. Used correctly, such an obvious principle can add a great deal of depth to your image.

Virtually every project in this book makes use of these principles. Photoshop has a number of tools that rely on these principles and allow you to create amazing 3D effects in almost no time. ■

As you start to add the highlights and shadows always keep in mind where your light is coming from. The light source I use in this project is upper right and slightly behind the figure. This means Zaan is largely backlit and will have strong highlights only on his right side. Take another look at the finished illustration (**FIGURE 1-13**). This lighting should add drama to the scene, projecting Zaan forward as though he is coming from a place of fire and power. The main light source is very warm, meaning the highlights will be warm and the shadows cool. Since Zaan is largely lit from behind, a secondary light source will help add a sense of 3D. The secondary light source is the blue-green color on the left. This cool reflected light creates secondary highlights on the left of the figure. Whenever possible it's good to play warm against cool in this way. It not only makes the object *turn* and look more dimensional, but also when you combine cool colors with warm, you get a richer image.

FIGURE 1-13

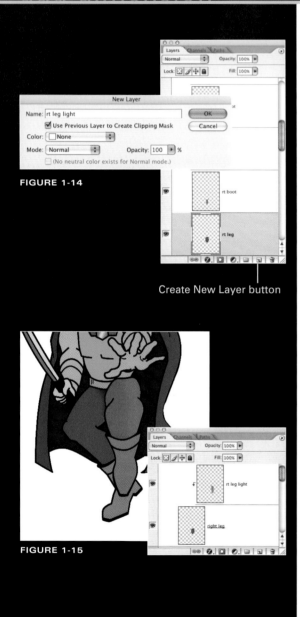

FIGURE 1-14

Create New Layer button

FIGURE 1-15

Let's start putting Layer clipping masks to work.

1. Click *right leg* in the Layers palette to make it the active layer. Option/Alt-click the *Create New Layer* button (**FIGURE 1-14**).

2. In the dialog, name the new layer *rt leg light* and check the box labeled *Use Previous Layer to Create Clipping Mask*. Click OK. Notice how the new layer appears in the Layers palette. It is stepped over to the right and a little arrow points to the layer below, with its name underlined. Those three things tell you that this is a clipping mask group. The underlined layer below is clipping the one above. Anything you put on the upper layer will only show where it overlaps the layer below.

3. We will create the sense of illumination by lightening the leg in several stages. First, add a lighter red tone using a soft brush about 150 pixels in diameter and be sure Shape Dynamics is unchecked in the Brushes palette.

   ➤ Use the Eyedropper (hold Option/Alt to access the Eyedropper without switching tools) to sample the color of the right leg, then choose a color that is a little lighter and shift the Hue toward orange. This isn't for the brightest highlight. First you will lighten the right side of the leg a little, then you will add the hard highlight along the edge.

   ➤ Be sure the Airbrush option is selected (click the Airbrush button in the Brush options bar or press Shift-Option-P/Shift-Alt-P). Adjust the Flow to around 50. Using a reduced flow will help the new color blend with the existing color below it. Now paint along the right side of the leg. One nice feature is that you don't have to be all that careful. Since the layer below is clipping the layer you're on, your painting looks nice and clean. You can use the Move tool to slide the new paint layer left or right to get the proper effect (**FIGURE 1-15**).

4. Option/Alt-click the *New Layer* button again to make a new layer. Name this layer *rt leg hard lite* and check the *Use Previous Layer to Create Clipping Mask* box. Click OK. Notice this layer also uses *rt leg* as a clipping mask. One layer can act as the clipping mask for as many layers as you like, but at this point you can't have clipping masks within a clipping mask group.

5. Now add the bright highlight to the right side of the leg. Increasing the flow to 100 may help to make the color really pop (**FIGURE 1-16**). Use this same technique throughout the illustration to add lights and shadows. Again, you may find the Eyedropper useful to first sample the existing color then go to the Color Picker and modify the color appropriately.

The Gradient tool also works great with clipping masks.

1. Select the *inside cape* layer. Option/Alt-click the *New Layer* button. Name the layer *inside lighten* and check *Use Previous Layer to Create Clipping Mask*. By the way, if you forget to check that box, just press Command-Option-G/Ctrl-Alt-G in CS2 or Command-G/Ctrl-G in CS to set up the clipping mask group.

2. Choose the Gradient tool. In the tool's option bar (**FIGURE 1-17**), choose Linear Gradient from the Gradient Styles, then open the Gradient Editor. From the presets in the Gradient Editor choose *Foreground to Transparent*. This is one of those "gotchas": If you don't choose this option you won't get the results we're after.

3. Now, sample the inside cape color, go to the Color Picker, choose a color that is a little lighter, and shift the Hue toward blue. In the image window, start at the bottom edge of the cape and drag upward while holding the Shift key to constrain the tool to go perfectly vertical. Let go about half way up the cape. Instantly the illustration has more dimension (**FIGURE 1-18**). We will be using the Gradient tool again to create the background.

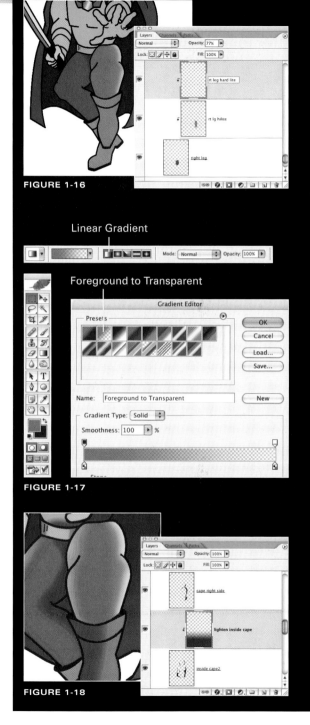

FIGURE 1-16

Linear Gradient

Foreground to Transparent

FIGURE 1-17

FIGURE 1-18

FIGURE 1-19

FIGURE 1-20

There's a neat trick to make the boots, armbands, and belt look like shiny metal.

1. Make a new layer above *rt boot*, using *rt boot* as a clipping mask.

   ➤ Set your color to bright yellow and with a small soft brush on 100% flow click the top of the boot. Let go and press the Shift key, move to the bottom of the boot and click again. Instantly you have a hard highlight running down the side of the boot (**FIGURE 1-19**).

   ➤ Repeat these steps on new layers for the armbands and belt.

Before you move on to the image background there is one piece of unfinished business. Back near the beginning I said I would show you a trick to make the lines thick again. Here it is: Highlight the Layer *zaan* and drag it to the top of the Layers palette (**FIGURE 1-20**). At first it will hide all the other layers. Don't panic. In the upper left corner of the Layers palette is the Layer blend modes menu. Blending modes affect the way a layer interacts with the layers below it. From that menu choose Multiply. Multiply will cause the darker colors to blend with the layers below, becoming even darker. Lighter colors will become increasingly transparent as they approach white. Pure white will disappear completely.

Make Zaan's world

To finish the illustration you will create a dramatic environment for our hero, something that contributes to the story and helps evoke that emotional response you're after. Don't get frustrated if yours doesn't end up looking exactly like the sample. Some of the techniques you will learn have unpredictable results and a couple of features that would be useful here won't be introduced until Project 2. But if you follow the steps outlined below you will end up with something very interesting—and have some fun in the process.

Imagine Zaan passing through a portal or entering another dimension. Here's an easy way to create a swirling, tunnel-like effect.

1. Choose the Gradient tool. Click the foreground color and set it to 100% yellow. Click the background color and set it to a bright red (100% magenta, 100% yellow).

   ➤ In the Gradient tool options bar, open the Gradient Editor and choose **Foreground to Background** (**FIGURE 1-21**). Click OK. For the Gradient style choose Radial.

   ➤ This time you are going to change the tool's blending mode. Normally, I don't mess with a tool's blending mode, mainly because I forget to change it back and get frustrated later when the tool doesn't act the way it's supposed to. Also, I prefer to play with blending modes in the Layers palette where they are nondestructive, but sometimes you can't get the effect you want any other way. So, from the Mode menu choose Difference.

   ➤ When creating a background for the image, it may be helpful at first to turn off all the other layers. You can do this by clicking the eye icon next to each group. That will automatically turn off everything inside the group. Layers not inside a group will need to be turned off individually.

2. Make a new group named BACKGROUND and move it to the bottom of the layer stack. Inside that group, make a new layer named *yel/red swirl*. In this group you will have a number of layers containing abstract colors and swatches of paint. Layers such as these become difficult to name, but do the best you can to come up with names that will help you identify them later.

   ➤ With the Gradient tool, start in the middle of the canvas and drag to any edge. (I chose yellow and red as the main elements of the background.) The image is filled with a smooth radial gradient transitioning from yellow to red.

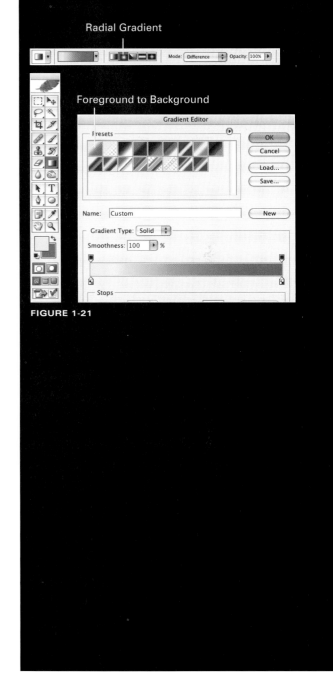

Radial Gradient

Foreground to Background

FIGURE 1-21

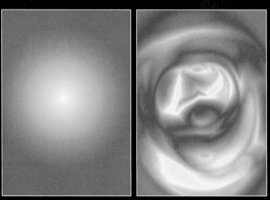

FIGURE 1-22

FIGURE 1-23

➤ Now do the same thing again *on the same layer*, but start at a slightly different point. Because the tool's blend mode is set to Difference the image goes completely black. No worries. Drag from the middle out again, starting in a slightly different spot than before. The image changes back to color but now it has all these interesting concentric shapes. Do this a couple of times varying the length of the drag a little each time. Start over on a new layer and try it again. Think of creating a kind of tunnel out of which Zaan is emerging (**FIGURE 1-22**).

➤ After you have something you like, turn all the groups back on and see what the total illustration looks like. Drag the layers you don't like to the trash at the bottom of the Layers palette.

SHARPEN THE FOCUS

Whenever you create an illustration or an ad, you want to try to keep the viewer's attention inside the ad, focused on what you consider most important. Here you want the viewer to focus on your hero, Zaan. The abstract concentric shapes that emerged in the last step are doing this to a degree. Now, you will make a series of layers to enhance this effect and help your character stand out against the vibrant background. You will use the Brush tool and work with curved strokes. If you are comfortable with using the Brush's Shape Dynamics, turning it on could help get the effect you need. (If you are not proficient with brushes, you might take time out now to do **Mini-Tutorial 1.1** at the end of this project.)

The colors you use and where you put them will depend on the colors you chose for Zaan's clothes and how your background has turned out thus far. If you haven't already done so, turn the other layers back on so you can see how Zaan looks against the background. The idea is to integrate him with the environment while separating him from the background enough to keep him from getting lost or overpowered by it. He needs to be integrated and yet stand out at the same time. Contrast is key here: Try to put light next to dark and warm next to cool where possible.

1. To create background contrasts similar to those shown here, make a new layer above *yellow swirl* and name it *rt yel light*. Use a soft brush with a Flow of about 40, and work in a circular motion to make an area of bright yellow just right of center (**FIGURE 1-23**). This tells the viewer where the primary light is coming from.

2. Make another layer and add deep red behind the right shoulder, to separate that side of the hood from the background.

3. On another layer paint a patch of yellow behind the left shoulder (**FIGURE 1-24**).

FIGURE 1-24

4. Blurring the layers softens the effect and helps them blend in with the layers below. Go to Filter > Blur > Gaussian Blur. Click OK when you are happy with the effect. One advantage of putting these colors on separate layers is that you can easily modify them. If your paint layers look too heavy-handed, try lowering the Layer Opacity.

5. Add one more layer and paint a bright, almost-white irregular shape in the upper right. That is the primary light source.

6. The image needs a blue-green secondary light source for the cool highlights on the left of Zaan to make sense. To get the effect shown here use two layers: the first a green irregular border down the left side (*lt grn border*), then one with a swath of aqua blue (*cool light source*) (**FIGURE 1-25**).

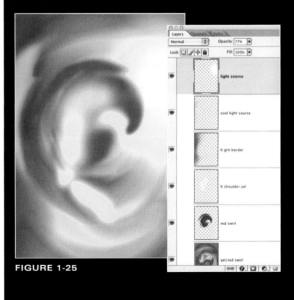

FIGURE 1-25

   ➤ You can use the Eraser tool on a soft brush setting to shape the painted areas. This is the only time I will suggest the Eraser. I never use it on important work because it is destructive.

   ➤ Blending modes will also help you blend these elements with the background. Try setting Layer *cool light source* to blending mode Pin Light. It is difficult to predict exactly how a layer will blend with the layers below. The effect

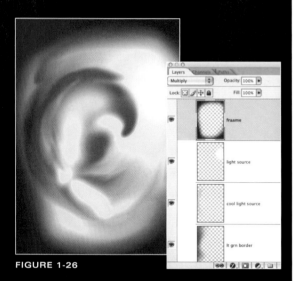

FIGURE 1-26

varies depending on the values and hues of the lower layers and whether or not those layers are themselves using blending modes. Without the layer *lt grn border*, for example, when the *cool light source* is put on Pin Light, the result is a bright off-white rather than blue. If your image doesn't look like the sample there are a couple of things you can try; use *lt grn border* as a clipping mask for *cool light source*, leave the blending mode on Normal and lower the Layer Opacity, try changing the blending mode to Color. Try to incorporate some of the colors of Zaan's clothes into the background. If done very subtly this will help give the entire image a unified look. Continue to fine-tune the background using additional paint layers. In the next project you will learn about layer masks. They give you much more control over these modifications and are completely nondestructive

7. Darken the outer edges to frame the illustration and draw attention to the center.

    ➤ Make a new layer named *frame*. Use a soft brush about 200 pixels in diameter and choose a dark red-brown color. Paint around the edge of the image, cutting the corners and creating an oval opening (**FIGURE 1-26**).

    ➤ Set this layer's blending mode to Multiply.

STRENGTHEN SHAPE WITH SHADOW

An earlier sidebar discussed the importance of cast shadows. Giving your hero a cast shadow will anchor him to the ground, add drama, and help define the light source.

1. Make a new layer at the top of the BACKGROUND group and name it *cast shadow*. Paint the shadow freehand or use the click, shift, move-and-click technique discussed in **Mini-Tutorial 1.1**. When using the brush, lower the flow to about 35%. This will allow you to build up the density of the shadow gradually

(**FIGURE 1.27**). As you learned earlier, an object's cast shadow is darkest at the point where the object meets the ground. In the next project you will learn how to use layer masks to gently blend elements such as this into the background.

➤ Blur the shadow and set its blend mode to Multiply.

➤ Lower the Opacity to about 80.

2. Once the background is created you may feel the colors of Zaan's clothes need to be modified. You can quickly change the color of a layer by using the Hue and Saturation command. Go to Image > Adjustments > Hue and Saturation, to access the Hue and Saturation dialog (**FIGURE 1.28**).

3. Use the sliders to change the hue, saturation, and lightness. One bit of caution: Doing this directly to a layer does change the pixels and thus is destructive. In the next project you will learn about Adjustment Layers that let you do the same thing totally nondestructively. For now, go ahead and play around with it and see what happens. You can note the values in the boxes above the sliders, and return to them if things go badly.

Here's one more trick that will make your illustration sing.

1. Add a new layer at the top of the layer stack named *glint*.

2. We need a special brush preset for this procedure. With the Brush tool active, click the brush sample in the options bar to display the Brush Presets Picker.

3. Click the triangle in the upper right corner of the picker to open the Brush Presets Picker menu, and choose Assorted Brushes. A dialog will ask you whether you want the new library to replace your current brushes. Click Yes to replace them, or click Append to add the new brushes to your list.

4. Scroll down the list until you find the Starburst-Small preset. Double-click it to choose it and close the picker. Increase the brush size to 175 pixels. With the Airbrush option on and using white paint, click the middle of the sword and hold for about

FIGURE 1-27

FIGURE 1-28

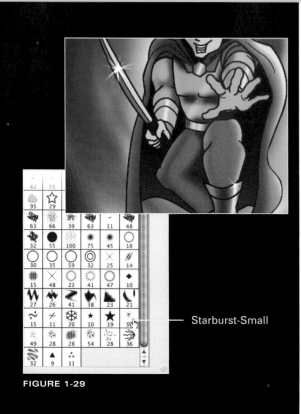

Starburst-Small

FIGURE 1-29

a second. Instantly you have made the sword glisten (**FIGURE 1.29**). Use a smaller brush size and do the same thing on the rim of the right boot. These little touches make a big difference, but be careful not to overdo them. They can start to look cheesy really fast.

Don't be afraid to experiment and have fun. *And remember to change the blend mode of your Gradient tool back to* **Normal**.

In this project you have learned some of the most fundamental, yet valuable tools and techniques Photoshop has to offer. Your time has been well spent, because this provides the foundation for everything else you learn from now on. Each project will introduce new tools and techniques that build on those learned in the previous projects. For example, in Project 2 you will learn among other things how to composite and manipulate images using layer masks and adjustment layers. These two features allow you to do amazing things nondestructively, but you can't use them effectively without understanding what you have learned here.

Not so long ago, we created ads the old way, with illustration board, acetate overlays, and real airbrushes. We inked crop marks indicating the ad's size on the board by hand. Layout artists then taped acetate overlays—usually several layers of them—to the foundation piece of illustration board. On one overlay we pasted an FPO (for position only) copy of the image to be used. The actual image was prepared on a separate board or in a high-priced photo lab. Another overlay contained the headline, and body copy was usually on another, separate overlay. This assembly was called a *mechanical*. The final photographic image was often prepared in the same way. In that case, a special acetate was used that could be painted on. The retouching artist used a number of overlays, dividing up the areas to be retouched. The reason everything was on separate overlays was to accommodate changes. That was as close as we came in those days to working nondestructively.

The developers of Photoshop used this process as a metaphor and constructed the Layers palette much like the old mechanical.

The Layers palette

The Layers palette looks deceptively simple. It contains an array of menus and buttons that conceal a deeply powerful and complex set of features and capabilities. Don't worry, you don't need to know how everything works right away. This is intended to give you a brief overview—these features will be discussed in detail over the course of the next three projects. The palette is divided into four sections. At the top are controls that let you choose the layer's blend mode and opacity, plus the Layers palette menu, indicated by the small triangle in the upper right corner. Below the controls are buttons that lock or protect objects on the layers in various ways. To the right of these buttons is the *fill* control. Then comes the section containing the actual layers. At the bottom are a series of buttons and icons that perform special functions, such as linking; or access special menus, like styles and fill/adjustment layers.

First, let's look at the layers section. Like the mechanicals of old, layers are built one on top of the other with the first layer (labeled *Background*) similar to the illustration board and the layers above similar to the acetate overlays (**PE 1.1A**). Objects on the topmost layer, the foreground, are closest to the viewer. There are six types of layers: *background*, *"normal,"* *fill*, *adjustment*, *shape*, and *smart object*. In this project you will be working with *background* and normal layers only. The others will be introduced in the next couple of projects and will be covered in detail then.

Every document must have at least one layer. When you make a new document, the first layer is always labeled *background*. It is italicized, indicating that it is special. Notice the white padlock icon next to the name. This tells you the layer is protected in some way. But be careful, the "protection" is very limited. Specifically, the *background* layer can't be moved to another position in the Layers palette, nor can it have a mask. It can, however, be modified in many other ways, most of which are destructive.

PE 1.1A

continues...

The *background* layer can be changed into a normal layer by double-clicking on the name and giving it a new name.

You can create new layers several ways. The two I find most useful are the keyboard shortcut, Shift-Command-N/Shift-Ctrl-N, and the ***Create a New Layer*** button at the bottom of the palette. The keyboard shortcut will open the *New Layer* dialog (**PE 1.1B**). Here you can give the layer a name. Naming layers is a good habit to learn, because it will make your document easier to work with down the line. If you click the Create a New Layer button a new layer will be automatically added and will be

named *Layer* followed by a number. Hold down the Option/Alt key when you click the button and you will get the New Layer dialog. You can rename a layer at any time by double-clicking its name and typing. The stacking order of layers can be changed simply by clicking on a layer and dragging it to a new position in the palette. The higher up a layer is in the stacking order, the closer the object on that layer will be to the viewer. In CS2 you can select multiple layers two ways: Shift-click two layers to select them and all layers in between. Command-click/Ctrl-click to select layers in any order. You can then drag all of the selected layers to a new position in the palette.

You can link layers to each other, which locks the objects on those layers together in the image window. They will move and scale in unison. Linking does not lock a layer's position in the Layers palette. Linked layers do not need to be sequential or in close proximity in the Layers palette. To link layers in CS2, highlight the layers you want to link, then click the link layers button at the bottom of the palette. A link icon will appear next to each of the linked layers (**PE 1.1C**). To unlink them, select the ones you want to remove from the link and click the link layers button again. In CS2 if you highlight multiple layers they will behave as if they are linked whether you click link icon or not, but that relationship is discontinued when the layers are no longer highlighted. To link layers in Photoshop CS, select one of the layers you want to include in the link, then click the link box (**PE 1.1D**) next to the name of each layer you want to add to the link. A link symbol will appear in the box. You may link as many layers together as you wish.

A layer can have masks, which allow you to conceal part or all of the objects on the layer without actually erasing any pixels. Masks allow you to create

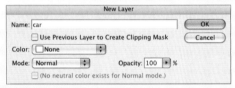

PE 1.1B

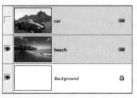

PE 1.1C

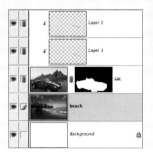

PE 1.1D

elaborate composites nondestructively. A layer can have a "regular" layer mask, a vector mask, or both (**PE 1.1E**). To add a layer mask, click the *Add Layer Mask* button  at the bottom of the palette. Click once to add a regular layer mask, click again to add a vector layer mask. Layer masks will be covered in detail in Project 2. Another type of mask, which you will use in this project, is a layer clipping mask. One layer is used to mask or clip part of the layer above it. The masking layer, together with the layers above it that are masked, constitute a "clipping mask" (**PE 1.1F**). In the New Layer dialog you can choose to **Use Previous Layer to Create Clipping Mask**. You can also create a layer clipping mask by highlighting the layer you wish to use as the mask and pressing Command-Option-G/Ctrl-Alt-G if you are working in CS2; and Command-G/Ctrl-G if you are using CS. In this project, you will use this technique to quickly add highlights and shadows to your illustration.

PE 1.1E

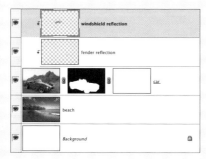

PE 1.1F

PE 1.1G

Now look at the top of the palette (**PE 1.1G**). On the left is the Blending Modes menu. Blending modes are a great way to instantly sex-up your document. A layer's blend mode affects the way its pixels interact with the pixels on the layers below it. Blend modes can transform the ordinary into the extraordinary by creating dramatic lighting effects or unexpected color interaction.

To the right of Blending Modes is the Opacity control. You can change the opacity of a single layer or the opacity of a group (*set* in CS), thereby changing the opacity of all layers inside the group.

In the next section, just below the Opacity control is the Fill Opacity control . At first, *fill opacity* seems no different from *opacity*. But, fill opacity comes in handy when you're working with layer styles. This won't make much sense until you understand styles, which will be covered in Project 3. Basically, the Fill Opacity control lets you reduce the opacity of an object without reducing the opacity of its style. This makes for some very cool effects.

To the left of the Fill Opacity control are a series of buttons that let you lock or protect certain aspects of a layer . The first one protects transparency, meaning that you can only edit the layer in areas where pixels already exist—the transparent area will remain transparent. The second one prevents objects on the layer from being modified by any of the painting tools, so you don't accidentally make destructive modifications. The third prevents objects on the layer from being moved, which is especially valuable if you are new to the program. It is easy, at first, to move objects unintentionally. The last button will perform all these functions at once.

continues…

At the bottom of the palette are a number of important buttons and icons. We have already discussed the Link Layers button, Add Layer Mask button, and Create a New Layer button. The circle with the *f* inside opens the Layer Styles menu. Layer Styles is an amazing and powerful feature that lets you instantly add and drop shadows, bevels, glows, and much more. You will use Layer Styles in Project 3. The half-black, half-white circle next to the Mask button opens the Fill and Adjustment Layers menu. Fill and adjustment layers are special layers that let you dramatically alter the appearance of an image totally nondestructively. You can use these to fine-tune the color or radically alter the appearance of an image. You will start using these features in Project 2 and they will, no doubt, become an important part of your Photoshop bag of tricks.

Next to the Create a New Fill and Adjustment Layers button is the *Create a New Group* button. in CS2 you can also create a group by selecting multiple layers and pressing Command-G/Ctrl-G—remember, *in CS this keystroke creates a clipping mask*. Groups (called *sets* in CS) are a way of organizing layers into collections. Groups

are very helpful for several reasons. First, as you add layers to your image, your Layers palette can grow to an awkward length. You can organize your layers into groups, then close the groups to reduce the number of layers displayed in the Layers palette (**PE 1.1H**). Also, certain attributes can be applied to a group, thus affecting every layer inside. The opacity or blend mode of a group can be changed, for example. A group can also have a mask, a huge time saver when you have multiple layers that require the same areas be concealed. You can have groups inside groups, but I would avoid this for the time being, as it can get very confusing.

At the bottom right is the trash can. Drag layers or masks here to eliminate them. Or simply highlight a layer and click the trash icon. To eliminate multiple layers, select them and click the trash icon.

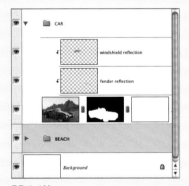

PE 1.1H

Graphics applications used to be divided into two categories, raster-based and vector-based. Paint applications such as Photoshop were essentially raster-based. Drawing programs such as Illustrator were vector-based. Today, the distinction is being blurred as vector-based tools and capabilities are being incorporated into Photoshop. But it is important to understand the difference between the two because it can greatly affect the way you work and the quality of the end product.

Raster-based technology is great for works with a specific number and size of pixels, forming a grid. This grid of pixels is referred to as either a bitmap or a raster, but Photoshop uses the term *bitmap* in a unique way, to mean an image made up of only black and white pixels. So *raster* has become the term most commonly used for images made up of pixels. If something is *rasterized* it has been assigned a specific number of pixels, each with specific qualities, such as depth, hue, saturation, and brightness. The number of pixels per linear inch determines the resolution of the document. If you increase the document's physical dimensions, the image size gets larger but the total number of pixels remains the same—they are just spread out over a larger area. So, for example, if you have a document that is 1″ x 1″ with a resolution of 100 pixels per inch (ppi) and increase the size to 2″ x 2″, you now have 50 pixels per linear inch. The resolution has been cut in half and so has the quality of the image. The image becomes softer, less focused. Taken to the extreme, you can actually begin to see the individual pixels and such an image is often referred to as *pixelated*. For this reason raster images are said to be *resolution dependent*. You can't increase the size without decreasing the quality.

Raster-based technology provides painting capabilities that are superior to those of vector-based technology.

Since a rasterized object is composed of a grid of pixels, edges are crisp and smooth as long as they are perfectly horizontal or vertical. But as soon as an edge becomes angled or curved the squares of the grid show up and the edges look jagged. To compensate for this Photoshop has a feature called *anti-aliasing*. When employed, this feature adds pixels of decreasing opacity along the outside edge of the object, making the edge appear smoother. The higher the resolution of the document, the smaller the pixels and the more effective anti-aliasing is. But even in hi-res documents, anti-aliased edges can't compete with the smooth, crisp edges achieved in vector objects.

With vector objects, what you see on your monitor is merely a representation of mathematical calculations. When you print the document, the resolution of the object is determined by the resolution of your printer. Since there isn't a fixed number of pixels and individual pixels have not been assigned any of the characteristics of rasterized objects, vector objects always have smooth, sharp edges and can be scaled as large as you like without a decrease in quality. Therefore, vector images are *resolution independent*.

Photoshop now gives you the best of both worlds. With the inclusion of vector-based tools such as the Type and Shape tools, you have all the painting and filtering capabilities available to rasterized objects combined with the ability to create crisp, smooth type and vector-based shapes.

mini-tutorial 1.1

Brushes

Brushes are among Photoshop's most useful and creative tools. Note that brushes are not restricted to the Brush tool: All of the painting tools except the Gradient tool use brushes. The number of *presets*—brushes designed by Adobe and included as standard in Photoshop—is impressive and the number of options available for creating custom brushes and modifying the presets is mind-boggling. To take full advantage of all these options you need a graphics tablet and stylus (pen). The tablets are pressure-sensitive and many of the options in the Brushes palette are designed with this in mind. A tablet is also a much more natural way to work than the mouse, and has the added advantage of reducing stress on your wrist and hand. Click the Brush icon in the toolbox to activate

the tool and bring up the tool's options bar. Photoshop provides several ways to choose and configure brushes. The most powerful of these is the Brushes palette, which (by default) is docked in the palette well at the right end of the options bar. You can also use the Brush Preset Picker on the left side of the options bar to access presets and make minor modifications.

Use the Brush Preset Picker to access a vast array of brush presets. To choose a brush preset, open the picker and click the preset you want to use. Modify its size and hardness as you like, using the sliders at the top of the palette. Use the Brush Preset Picker menu to change the way presets are displayed and to add more presets.

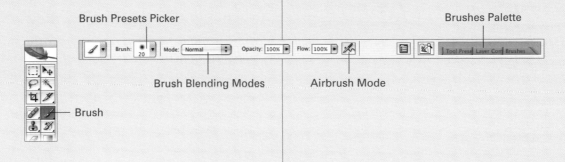

Brush Presets Picker

Brushes Palette

Brush Blending Modes

Airbrush Mode

Brush

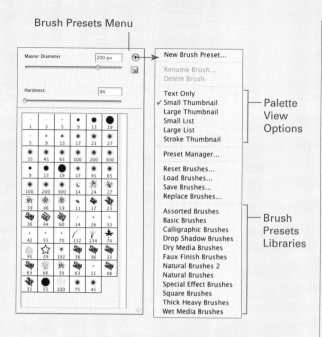

Brush Presets Menu

Palette View Options

Brush Presets Libraries

reduce the Flow the density of the color increases when you cross over an already painted area. For example, if Opacity is at 100% with Flow at 10% and you paint in a continuous motion, you can build up paint gradually, using just one stroke. With both Opacity and Flow reduced, in one stroke you can build up color over previously painted areas, up to but not beyond the level of the Opacity setting.

When working in standard brush mode, you can use your keypad to modify *Opacity*. When working in airbrush mode, the keypad numbers modify the *Flow*. To change Opacity or Flow to a multiple of 10, just type one number, for example type 2 to get 20%. Type two numbers if you want a quantity that's not a multiple of 10: type 34 to get 34%.

Tip: Hold down Shift while typing the numbers to affect the OTHER quantity. For example, if Airbrush is on, type Shift-3 to change the Opacity to 30%. If Airbrush is off, type Shift-7 to set the Flow to 70%.

The main difference between standard brush mode and airbrush mode is that if you click and hold when using the airbrush you will get a continuous flow of paint, much like holding down the nozzle on a spray can. The standard brush will give you just one shot. If you paint in a continuous motion, applying the same amount of pressure, the brushes behave essentially the same. I often use airbrush, however, because it allows me to build up paint gradually by reducing the speed of my stroke or over-painting without the need to lift the stylus and begin a new stroke.

Use the Mode menu to choose a blending mode for your brush. I usually leave this on *Normal,* preferring to make blending mode changes in the Layers palette. The next three options—Opacity, Flow, and Airbrush—require some explanation. Opacity regulates density—how dark the color can become in one stroke. If you reduce the opacity while using a standard brush, as long as you don't lift the stylus or let go of the mouse, the color won't get any darker even if you cross over your strokes. Flow regulates the amount of paint supplied to the brush.

Both controls can be used together in standard brush mode, with some interesting results. If you

THE PALETTE OF ABUNDANCE

By default, the Brushes palette is docked in the well. You can also press F5 to access it. This is one of Photoshop's most complex palettes. The number of options available in it is intimidating, but once you dig in and start playing around with them I think enthusiasm will soon replace intimidation.

This palette offers eight categories of options, with multiple options within each category. To access the parameters for each category, click on the words naming the category, not on the check box next to the words. Two categories, Brush Presets and Brush Tip Shape, do not have check boxes. Click the words *Brush Presets* to access the Brush Preset Picker. Click *Brush Tip Shape* to modify the diameter, shape, hardness, and spacing of a particular brush. Diameter (size) and shape are self-explanatory, but a few words about spacing may be in order.

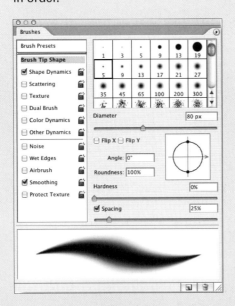

When you paint with a Photoshop brush using the default settings, it appears that you are getting a continuous smooth line. Actually, Photoshop applies the paint in a series of individual spots of color in the shape of the brush. Spacing determines how often a spot of paint is applied. If you increase the spacing you will begin to see the individual spots.

Of the six other categories, I have found four the most useful: Shape Dynamics, Scattering, Color Dynamics, and Other Dynamics. This tutorial will focus on these four.

In each of these four categories you will find an option called *jitter*, which basically means randomness. Increase jitter and you increase randomness. Below nearly every option is a menu called *Control*. Here you choose the means by which the option will be applied. You'll need a graphics tablet and stylus (pen) to take full advantage of everything the Brushes palette has to offer. The tablet takes some getting used to, but it is a much more natural way to paint, and by increasing or reducing pressure you can control how the effects are applied. If you have a tablet, Pen Pressure is often the Control choice to make. If you don't have a tablet, leave the control setting at Off or on Fade. Fade will cause whichever property you are modifying to be reduced and eventually disappear based on the pixel number you enter in the field next to the Control menu. For example, if you are modifying size and enter 25, the stroke will taper to a point and end 25 pixels from where it began. Now, let's take a look at each of the four categories. As we examine each one, check the box next to it and **click its name** to access the options associated with it.

Shape Dynamics

When Shape Dynamics is on, Pen Pressure is chosen in the Control menu by default. With all of the jitter factors at zero, you get a smooth tapering stroke. The idea is to simulate a real brush stroke, where you lightly touch the brush to the paper then apply more pressure and gently reduce pressure as you lift it off the paper. Later, when we get into using the Brush tool to work on layer masks, you may find you want to turn this feature off. You can change the default of any setting by clicking the lock symbol next to the item.

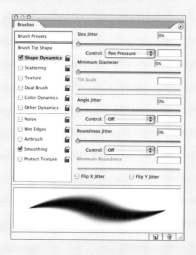

In this pane you can modify Size, Angle, and Roundness. The window at the bottom of the palette will show what the stroke will look like as you change the settings. I think Size is self-explanatory. Angle has no effect on a round brush, but many of the brushes are not round. Later in this tutorial we will be using a leaf brush. By adding jitter to Angle you can achieve a less uniform, more natural look. The leaves will tilt and turn randomly. Roundness jitter will vary the width of a brush. This can add a sense of 3D.

Scattering

When you paint, the brush deposits "paint" in individual spots of color. Scattering will spread the position of the spots around the stroke. Increasing Scatter moves the spots away from the stroke if Both Axes is not checked; if it is checked, the spots are scattered along the stroke as well as perpendicular to it. Use *Count* to increase or decrease the population of spots.

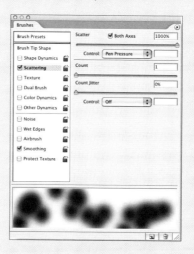

Color Dynamics

Use this option to vary the color of the stroke between the foreground and background or to add random changes to hue, saturation, and brightness. Increasing jitter in the first option, Foreground/Background, will cause the paint applied by your brush to alternate randomly between the foreground and background colors in your image. When you increase the Hue jitter you no longer restrict this transition to the foreground and background colors, but allow a much broader range of color depending on how much jitter you add. This can produce an unexpected and playful result. Adding jitter to Saturation affects the vividness of the color. Adding jitter to

Brightness modifies the overall lightness or darkness of the color. The Purity setting determines the highest degree of saturation your brush can produce.

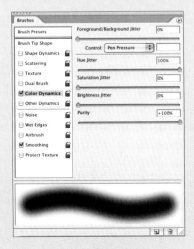

Other Dynamics

Here you can apply jitter to Opacity and Flow. I have found that increasing Opacity jitter gives me better results than increasing Flow jitter. Modifying both of them at the same time has not produced satisfactory results for me.

Below these categories are five options that affect the way the paint is applied. Airbrush and Smoothing are the ones I use most often. Sometimes I will use Wet Edges to get a watercolor look. This one can also add an organic quality to a stroke.

THE EXERCISE

Open the image **MT_1-1.psd** from the CD or your hard drive. (You *did* copy the CD images to your hard drive as suggested in the Introduction, didn't you?) This file contains the scan of a book cover my son made, which appears in the Layers palette as the background layer, named *bookcover*. We will use it to explore some of the options just discussed. Painting with brushes on multiple layers below and above this *bookcover* layer will create something reminiscent of a Japanese print. Within the group LEAF SCAN is the scanned image of a leaf I found in the garden. We will use this to create a custom brush. **Each step of this tutorial should be done on a separate layer.** The undo key commands will also be a big help. Command-Z/Ctrl-Z will undo the last thing you did. Command-Option-Z/Ctrl-Alt-Z allows you to make multiple undos.

1. First, hide *bookcover* by clicking the eye next to the layer name. Make a new layer and name it *red field*. Choose a bright red color from the Color Picker. You can do this visually or by entering specific percentages in the CMYK fields. A good bright red consists of C=0%, M=100%, Y=100%, and K=0%. The CMYK percentages in this tutorial are offered only as helpful guides; the actual color choices are yours to make. After you have chosen the foreground color, fill the layer (Option-delete/Alt-Backspace).

> ➤ Drag this layer below *bookcover*. Getting a layer to insert below the first layer is a little tricky sometimes. I have found it helps if you aim slightly to the left rather than dragging straight down. If this doesn't work, try dragging *bookcover* above *red field*.

2. Now add two layers above red field. Name one *red snake* and the one above it *yellow snake*. Choose a large soft brush—about 300 pixels should work. You can change brush sizes quickly by pressing the square bracket keys on your keyboard. The right bracket enlarges the

brush size and the left decreases it. Airbrush should be on with the flow at 100%. Shape Dynamics should be on with all the settings at 0%. If you are working with a tablet, choose Pen Pressure from the Control menu.

3. Paint undulating snake-like forms across the image using a dark red color (C=5%, M=100%, Y=100%, K=28% is good) on *red snake* layer and an ochre-yellow (C=0%, M=29%, Y=93%, K=0% works well) on *yellow snake* layer. It may be easier to get a nice smooth stroke if you zoom out a bit.

> ➤ As you paint the strokes, vary the pressure on the stylus to change the width of the stroke. The curves on the two layers should not match, but should overlap in places. You may need to try this several times to get a nice fluid stroke. Press Command-Z/Ctrl-Z to redo a stroke, or make new layers and try it several times. Drag the layers you don't want to keep to the trash.

➤ Blur each layer by choosing Filter > Blur > Gaussian Blur and entering a setting of 30 pixels in the Radius field.

4. Set the *red snake* layer to Multiply mode and choose Linear Dodge for the *yellow snake* layer. Show *bookcover* (click the box next to the layer name) and set its blending mode to Multiply.

5. Open the Brushes palette menu. Load the library called Natural Brushes. When you highlight Natural Brushes and release, you will be asked if you want to replace the current set or append it by adding the new collection of brushes. Choose Append.

➤ From this set choose Charcoal 41 pixels. In the set, it may be helpful to temporarily change the display to Large List to help you find the preset. It looks like a rectangle made up of a lot of little dots.

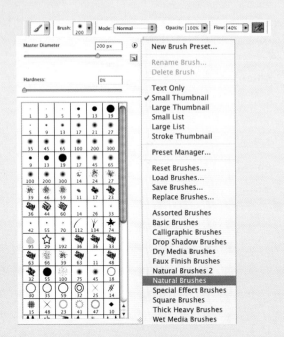

➤ Increase the Master Diameter to 100 pixels, turn on Airbrush and lower the flow to 25%. Choose a bright yellow-ocher color (C=0%, M=37%, Y=94%, K=0%).

6. Make a new layer **above** *bookcover* and name it *yellow dry brush*. Make quick, broad strokes on the left side of the image. The idea is to get the look of paint applied with a semi-dry brush so the brush strokes are really noticeable. You may need to try this a few times on different layers until you have something you like. When you are satisfied, drag the layers you don't want to the trash and change the blending mode of the remaining layer to *hard light*.

Save your document.

7. Next, you will create similar brush-like strokes that appear to go behind the Chinese calligraphic character in the center of the image (We'll call this character *Kanji,* the Japanese word for this type of writing). Normally, I would do this using a layer mask, but since we haven't covered layer masks yet, you'll use the Magic Wand. Click the Magic Wand and set the tolerance to 32. Be sure to check Sample All Layers.

➤ Temporarily hide layers *red snake* and *yellow snake* in order to get a good selection. Click inside the red area surrounding Kanji to load that area as a selection.

➤ On a new layer named *kanji dry brush,* use the brush preset Charcoal 41 and the same yellow color as in the last step and quickly paint five or six strokes at different angles to one another on the right side of the selection. Deselect (Command-D/Ctrl-D).

8. Next, we'll create a custom brush. Make the LEAF SCAN group visible by clicking the box just left of the set name. An eye will appear in the box. Press Option/Alt and click the eye to hide all of the other layers at one time.

➤ Highlight the layer *leaf* and Command/Ctrl-click on the thumbnail of the leaf in the Layers palette. This will load the leaf as a selection.

➤ Go to Edit > Define Brush Preset. In the dialog, name the brush *leaf* and click OK. The image of the leaf has now been added to your brush presets.

➤ Option/Alt-click the eye next to the group name to turn the other layers back on. Now that you are finished creating the custom brush, you no longer need that group on. Click the eye again to hide the group.

THE MAGIC OF CUSTOM BRUSHES

Now, we will add falling leaves. You definitely want to use different layers for this since the results are unpredictable. Putting the leaves on different layers gives you flexibility to edit, change blending modes, and modify opacity. You will be using the custom brush you created from the scan. A very nice leaf shape is one of Photoshop's presets, but it is very flat. The scanned leaf will add an organic feel. Using layers of different value and hue can add a sense of depth. When doing this you should usually start with the darkest colors first.

For dramatic effect, your first layer of leaves here will be black. You will add several layers of colored leaves above that but the color palette will be very narrow—everything on the warm side of the spectrum. This will emphasize the autumn theme and create a feeling of drama and intensity.

A FEW WORDS ABOUT LAYER BLENDING MODES

Layer blending modes affect the way the pixels on one layer interact or blend with pixels on the layers below. The beauty of Layer blending modes is that they are completely nondestructive. The blending modes I use most often are Multiply, Color Burn, Color Dodge, Linear Dodge, Soft Light, and Hard Light. But I recommend you play around with all of them to get a feel for what they do. Multiply combines the darkest areas of the top layer with the darkest areas of the layers beneath, while preserving the tonality of those layers. Areas of the top layer that have a value of 50% or lighter will become less opaque, with white areas disappearing completely. Color Burn produces a similar effect but with interesting color shifts and a "burnt edge" quality. Color Dodge works the opposite of Multiply. It combines the brightest areas of the layers causing a blown-out effect. Color Dodge often results in hard edges, Linear Dodge will produce a similar but smoother effect. Soft Light and Hard Light will intensify the darkest darks and lighten the lightest lights. Soft Light is often too subtle and Hard Light too strong. Refer to **Photoshop Essential 1.1: Layers** to learn how to use opacity to regulate the effect of blending modes. ∎

1. Press D (Default) to return the foreground and background colors to black and white. From the brush presets choose the leaf brush that you created from the scan. Reduce Master Diameter to about 350 pixels.

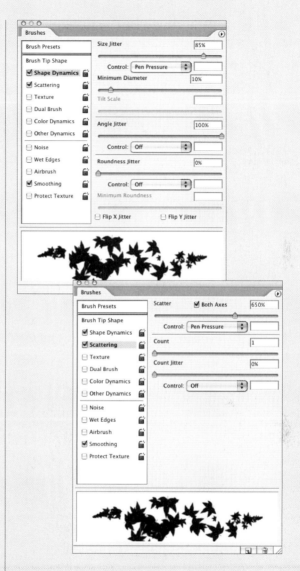

➤ By using Size jitter, you will get leaves of different sizes automatically, 350 pixels is the size of the largest leaf the brush creates. In Shape Dynamics choose Pen Pressure from the Control menu. Set the Size Jitter to 85%. The size of the leaves will be determined by the amount of pressure you apply to the stylus. Set the Minimum Diameter to 10%.

➤ To create a natural falling look, you want the angle of the leaves to vary randomly. To achieve this, set the Angle Jitter to 100%.

To spread the leaves out, you need to increase the scatter. Check the box next to Scattering and click the word *Scattering* to view the options. Increase Scatter to 650%. Check Both Axes and choose Pen Pressure from the Control menu. Choosing Pen Pressure will give you more control over where the leaves go. If you are using a mouse or have Off choosen from the Control menu, the leaves will be scattered randomly across the image. Leave Count at 1 and Count Jitter at 0%.

2. Make a new layer named *blk leaves* above *kanji dry brush*. With the Opacity and Flow set at 100% make a curved stroke from the lower left to the upper right. When you are using jitter, the results are always unpredictable—that's the whole point. You will have a little more control if you make your stroke slowly rather than quickly, as you did when creating the dry brush effect.

➤ Begin at the top center and slowly paint down the left side. Vary the pressure to get a variety of sizes and shades of yellow and orange. Add another layer and do the same thing down the right side. Use the Move tool to move the leaves on these layers to the outside, if necessary, so that not too much of *Kanji* is obstructed.

4. To finish the illustration we will add a soft black frame. Press D to set the foreground and background colors back to black and white. Choose a soft round brush about 80 pixels in diameter. Zoom out and drag the document window open so you have some room to work.

3. Now, pick a bright yellow for the foreground (C=0%, M=17%, Y=93%, K=0%) and orange (C=0%, M=78%, Y=98%, K=0%) for the background. In Color Dynamics set Foreground/Background Jitter to 100%. Purity should be 100%. The other settings should remain the same as in the last step.

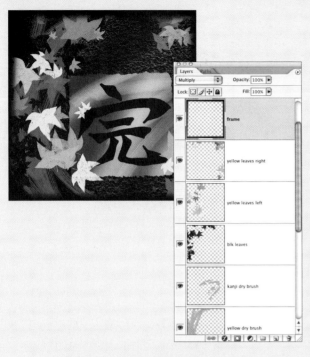

OPTIONS UNLEASHED

In this example I made a custom brush preset from my intials, then set the following Brush palette options.

➤ **Shape Dynamics**: Size Jitter 100%, Minimum Diameter 0%, Angle Jitter 100%.

➤ **Scatter**: Scatter Jitter 100%.

➤ **Color Dynamics**: Hue Jitter 100%.

Then on one layer I made a few strokes, varying the pressure as I went. That produced the type in various sizes and colors, and at all the wacky angles. On another layer, using the same brush, but with all the option boxes unchecked, I painted the yellow letters, using the square brackets to increase and decrease the brush diameter.

➤ Click in the upper left corner, press the Shift key, move to the upper right corner, and click again. You will get a straight stroke between the points where you clicked. Continue to hold down the Shift key and click in each of the remaining corners. With just four clicks you have created a frame around your composition. Set the blending mode to Multiply. Remember this technique, because it will be very useful later on.

This brief tutorial is merely an introduction to the capabilities of the Brush tool. There is no end to the creative possibilities. What you have created here is based on a very limited color palette. The dark warm colors evoke a rather quiet, somber feeling. By simply changing a few options you can instantly create something playful and energetic.

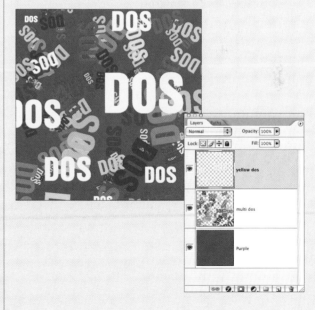

mini-tutorial 1.2

Gradients

There's an industry term, "Adding production value,"that means making a production appear bigger, more impressive, more expensive. As a designer, your goal is to add maximum production value to your graphics for minimum cost and effort. One of Photoshop's most effective tools for accomplishing this is the Gradient tool.

Gradients are gradations or transitions from one color or value to another. The gradations can be based on various parameters, such as hue (from green through blue to purple, for example), or opacity (from more transparent to more opaque), or value (lighter to darker)—or all of these. The way these gradations behave is largely determined by the Gradient style (Linear, Radial, Angle, Reflected, Diamond) and the tool's blending mode.

With all of these parameters, the possibilities are virtually limitless. To make life easy, Photoshop starts you off with a number of presets to choose from, which you can use as-is or modify; but you can also create and save your own custom gradients.

In this mini-tutorial, you'll explore some of these possibilities. The goal here is not necessarily to

create a finished-looking piece of art, but to introduce you to the capabilities of this remarkable tool and get your creative juices flowing.

THE GRADIENT EDITOR

The Gradient Editor is the key to getting the most out of this tool. Let's take a look at how it works. Choose the Gradient tool and examine the options bar. In the options bar just to the right of the tool icon is the Gradient Preview. This displays the currently selected gradient. Click on it to open the Gradient Editor.

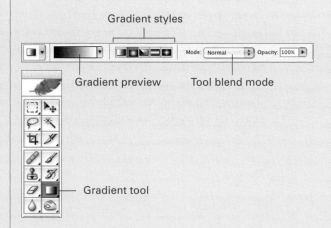

Gradient styles

Gradient preview   Tool blend mode

Gradient tool

The Gradient Editor comprises two main sections. At the top are the Gradient Presets, with thumbnails of all the currently available gradients.

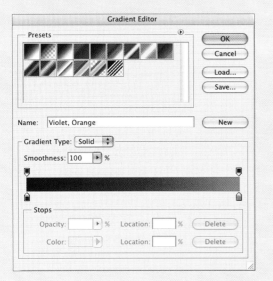

Three of the gradients, the first two and the last, are exceptions in that they rely on the current foreground and background colors, not predetermined colors. Choose the first one to make a gradient that transitions from the foreground color to the background color, creating a gradient that fills the entire area. Choose the second one to create a gradient that transitions from the foreground color to transparent. The last gradient in the default collection of presets uses the current foreground color to create a striped effect.

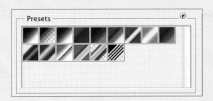

Below the Gradient Presets are the parameter controls where editing takes place. Here you see the Gradient bar, which displays the current gradient and shows how the gradient is constructed. Along the bar are small controls called *stops*—opacity stops along the top, color stops along the bottom—each indicating the point on the gradient where the parameter takes effect. Slide them back and forth along the bar to create different types of gradients.

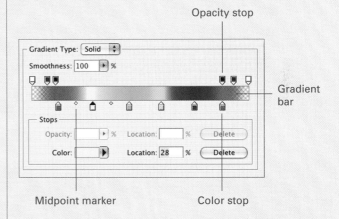

You can add more stops simply by clicking near the bar; to delete a stop, click it and drag it away from the bar. To change a color, click the appropriate stop and either access the Color Picker by clicking the field next to the word *color* in the *stops* panel below the bar, or by moving your pointer over the bar, at which point the pointer becomes the eyedropper and you can sample a color from the bar.

The small diamonds between the stops are midpoint markers, representing the point at which the two colors on either side of the marker mix in exactly equal amounts. Use these to modify how the colors are distributed along the gradient. With these you can create gradations that are long and gradual, very abrupt, or anything in between. Click a few of the presets to see how the stops along the bar and the values associated with them change.

All right, let's see how this stuff really works.

WORKING WITH GRADIENTS

Create a new document 5 x 7 inches, RGB at 150 ppi. Make your foreground color a deep blue and the background a lighter blue-green. Choose the Gradient tool. In the options bar click the Gradient Preview to open the Gradient Editor.

Select the first preset, Foreground to Background, and click OK. Choose Linear gradient from Gradient styles and be sure Mode is set to Normal. Opacity should be 100%.

Full-frame linear gradient

Holding down the Shift key, begin at the top of the document, drag to the bottom, and release. The Shift key constrains the angle of the gradient, keeping it perfectly vertical. A gradient that goes from the foreground color to the background color now fills the entire image.

Radial gradient that fades to transparent

Make a new layer. Change the foreground color to rich purple. Select Radial from the Gradient styles and **Foreground to Transparent** in the Gradient Editor. Drag from the center of the image to about half an inch from the edge of the canvas, and release. You now have a radial gradient emanating from the center of the image, fading gradually to reveal the layer below.

Tip: It's best to do these gradients on separate layers so you can move them around or trash one if you don't like the results.

A glowing sphere

1. This involves the same technique as in the previous step, but by changing the color you will create the illusion of 3D. First, you need to change the foreground color to white. (To do this quickly, press the D key to reset the foreground and background colors to their defaults—black and white. Then press the X key to swap the foreground and background colors. Now, the foreground color is white.)

2. On a new layer, use the Gradient tool and drag, as in the previous step, from the center to near the edge. Because you have chosen Foreground to Transparent, the color is more opaque in the center of the image, creating the sense of a highlight and the illusion of 3D.

CUSTOMIZE A GRADIENT PRESET

1. Start by selecting the orange-yellow-orange preset (second from the end on the top row of presets). Now, you will customize the gradient by moving the opacity and color stops.

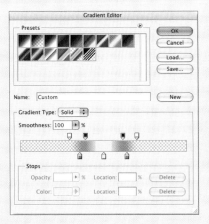

2. First move the opacity stops (on top of the bar) toward the center as shown. Add new opacity stops on each end of the bar by clicking on or near the top side of the bar. Make the opacity of these stops 0% and slide them toward the center. This will cause the gradient to transition from opaque to transparent. The closer the 0% opacity stops are to the 100% stops, the more abrupt the transition will be.

3. Next, move the color stops toward the center as shown. This will restrict the light area to the center part of the gradient. The brightest part will be right in the center creating a highlight effect. Click OK.

Golden cones

1. Now you'll use the custom gradient you just created to make two golden cones. Select the Angle gradient from the options bar.

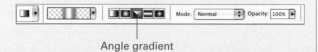

Angle gradient

2. On a new layer, hold down the Shift key and drag with the Gradient tool from the center of the canvas to the top edge. Because you are using the Angle gradient, where the color appears may be a surprise—opposite of what you might expect.

3. Make another new layer and repeat the procedure, but this time drag from the center down to the lower edge of the canvas. You now have two golden cones opposite one another. The angle gradient is creating the cone shape, and the changes you made to the color stops are creating the highlight and the 3D effect. The new 0% opacity stops are causing the gradient to abruptly become transparent, creating the cone effect.

4. Without these new opacity stops the orange would completely fill the image area. Having the cones on different layers allows you to reposition them. Try moving them away from one another slightly to increase tension and to allow the other layers to show through in the center. This creates a greater sense of depth.

ADD A NEW GRADIENT TO THE PRESETS

1. Again, starting with an existing preset, you will create a custom gradient and this time you will save it as a new preset. The order in which a new preset is made and saved is a little counterintuitive. First, you create the gradient, then you name it, then you click new.

2. To get started, open the Gradient Editor and select the Blue-Yellow-Blue preset (third from the right). Slide the two outer color stops toward the center and add two new color stops on each side of the bar—one on each end and one about halfway between the ends and the stops you just moved. You add new color stops by clicking on or near the bottom edge of the

bar. You should have a total of seven color stops at this point.

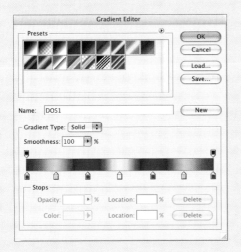

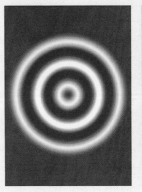

3. Change the color of the stops second from each end to gold and the end stops to red. Leave the opacity stops at 100%. Now, name the gradient. The name doesn't matter much, as you will be using its thumbnail (not its name) to select it in the future. I named mine DOS1. Click *New*.

4. A thumbnail of the gradient now appears in the Presets pane and will remain a preset of your application until you delete it or reset the application's preferences. Click OK to close the Gradient Editor.

Layer blending mode

1. Make a new layer and select Radial gradient from the options bar. As before, drag out from the center, and release about half an inch from the edge of the canvas. Because the gradient is 100% opaque, the entire image area is covered by the new gradient.

2. To allow the other layers to show through and create a soft, ethereal effect, change the layer blend mode to Soft Light (the Layers blend mode menu is at the top left of the Layers palette).

Hard-edged, striped gradient

1. Make your foreground color black (press the D key) and open the Gradient Editor. As mentioned earlier, the last gradient of the presets (now second from last, since you added a custom gradient) creates stripes. Click its thumbnail to make it the current gradient.

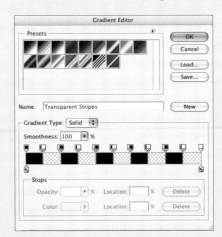

2. Look at the Gradient bar and notice how this gradient has been created. There are opaque areas separated by totally transparent areas. The transition between the two is very abrupt. This will produce an almost hard-edged stripe effect. The color is black because it is based on your current foreground color. Click OK to close the Gradient Editor.

3. Make sure Radial is still selected in the options bar and drag out from the center, releasing about a quarter of an inch from the edge of the canvas. At first, you have a series of black concentric circles, but change the Layer blending mode to Soft Light and the circles become light and blend with the other layers.

A FINISHING TOUCH

I often use some type of a framing device on my images. I feel it makes the piece look more finished and helps to draw the viewer into the image. The frame needn't be a well-defined shape like a picture frame—it can be as simple as a subtle darkening of the color in the corners and along the edges.

1. Choose Linear gradient from the options bar. Change the foreground color to dark blue. In the Gradient Editor select Foreground to Transparent and click OK.

2. On a new layer, start in the upper left corner and drag toward the center. Release about halfway from the corner of the canvas frame to the center. Repeat this on new layers for each corner. This will darken the corners and make the center of the image stand out. Adjust the opacity to suit you and experiment with different layer blend modes. The effect can be very subtle or quite dramatic.

Gradients immediately add a sense of illumination and dimension to any image or design. Whether working on a print job or motion graphics for an on-air promotion, I find myself constantly using gradients. And, as you will discover in Project 2, gradients are invaluable tools for masking.

The Most Watched Weekly News Magazine.
Ever.*

Our World is the highest rated news magazine in the history of television.

In fact, during the first quarter more people watched **Our World** than all other news magazines combined.

MATT WILLIS

LISA DEREYES

VINCE HARCOURT

Wour WORLD cTV MON 7PM

magazine
ad

AD MAGAZINE AD MAGAZINE AD **MAGAZINE AD.**

IN THIS PROJECT YOU WILL CREATE A MAGAZINE PRINT AD.

Most print ads fall into either of two categories, *consumer* or *trade*. The difference between them is important for you, the artist, to understand because rarely does a digital artist today deal with only the image. More often than not, you will also be the designer. To design an effective ad, you need to understand its purpose and its target. Consumer ads are aimed directly at the end user, the consumer, while trade ads may be thought of as business-to-business advertising. Both have the same ultimate goal—to generate revenue by increasing sales—and in the past there was a clear visual distinction between the two. Consumer ads tended to be more visually stimulating, while trade ads were more straightforward, down-to-business looking. Today trade ads look more like consumer ads, but the stories they tell and the emotions they elicit are quite different.

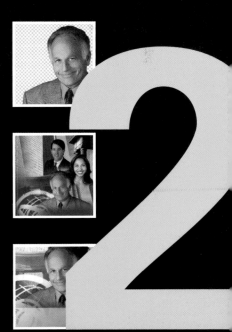

2

CONSUMER ADS

are more personal, appealing to the *individual's* needs and wants. Their goal is to drive sales by making you, the consumer, feel that "this movie is going to entertain me by letting me experience vicarious adventure, sex, violence, love" or "this product will make me feel more attractive, more successful, give me more of the lifestyle I deserve." Consumer ads can also appeal to your sense of responsibility or security, by making you feel guilty for not calling your mother or investing in a college fund. The bottom line is, consumer ads attempt to convince you that if you buy or do a particular thing, you are going to feel or be better in some way. During the creative development of a consumer ad, either the headline or the image may drive the direction of the ad. The headline may come first, then an image must be developed around it; or the image may come first and a headline must be found that goes with it. Either way, in the end, a successful consumer ad will have a compelling image supported by a smart, witty, or intriguing headline—and the emotional aspect will be apparent.

TRADE ADS

increase sales and generate revenue in a different way. The target audience is usually not the individual consumer, but rather other companies. Trade ads carry a business message and seek a business response. There are several types of trade ads, each approaching the goal of generating revenue differently. Most trade ads for *television* attempt to increase revenue by boosting the sale of on-air advertising time. These ads try to convince the media buyers and advertising planners for retail companies that a particular show or network will deliver more viewers of a specific demographic than its competitors will. If that demographic matches their client's target audience, the media buyers and planners will buy air time on that network or station. This type of trade advertising is all about *ratings*. Companies such as Nielsen Media Research monitor how many people watch a particular show and then assign the show a number (the rating)—a percentage of the total viewing population. The ratings can be broken down into subgroups, such as *males 18 to 24*. The ratings number is very important, because ratings determine how much a television station or network can charge for the air time. Ads of this type will appear in industry publications such as *The Hollywood Reporter* or *Daily Variety*. These ads generally will make a strong statement, presenting a show's rating in the best possible light. Example headlines might be: **Most-Watched Show in America**; **Number One Among Women**; **Record-Breaking**. The idea is to get attention by making the strongest claim possible, but these claims must be supported by the actual research. The headline will often be followed by an asterisk that references the source of the claim in small type at the bottom of the ad. In this kind of ad the headline must be compelling and the image must support it. As with all advertising, trade ads do play to emotions, but in a subtler, more businesslike way. Sometimes they will include charts or bullet points to drive home their ratings claims. Design is secondary to the message.

AWARDS-RELATED TRADE ADS

make up a significant portion of entertainment trade advertising. Getting a major award such as an Emmy for a television show or an Oscar for a movie is very important. A major award for a television show will almost always boost ratings immediately, and for a movie it will increase ticket sales. The industry spends an enormous amount of time, energy, and money campaigning for these awards, in ads directed at a small but powerful group of people—the voting members of the organizations that give the awards. These ads flood the industry publications near nominations time and again near voting time. Special issues are devoted to the awards campaigns, with covers purchased to promote particular shows or actors. The goal is to keep a show, its cast, and its crew on the voting members' minds and convince them of the show's merits. At FX Networks, I designed many ads that were intended to secure a nomination for an Emmy award. If a show or actor did get a nomination, another ad series was run with the intention of persuading members to give the nominee their vote. If the award was won, another ad series was run congratulating the show or actor and thanking the members for their votes.

IMAGE or BRANDING

ads, another important type of advertising, can be either consumer or trade ads. Their purpose is to reinforce brand awareness, promote a particular aspect of a network's brand, and give the brand a *sense of place*. In consumer advertising the branding ad will try to convince you that this network is where you belong; it has what people like you are interested in. In trade advertising, the same ad, or a slight variation of it, will convey the message to certain advertisers that this network delivers the audience that will buy their client's product. TNT's brand message, *we know drama*, for example, is driven home in both consumer and trade advertising. Consumer advertising's purpose is to persuade viewers to turn to TNT for dramatic entertainment. Trade advertising's purpose is to convince media buyers that people who watch TNT fit into a particular demographic. Another example is CNN, which claims to have more affluent viewers than FOX News. If you are a media planner for the agency representing Mercedes-Benz, CNN wants you to know this. These ads might appear in *Adweek*, *AdAge*, and *The Wall Street Journal*. If you are a consumer, CNN wants you to know that when it comes to delivering the news, educated, upper-income people find more of what they are looking for at CNN. These ads would likely be placed in *The New York Times* business section or high-end consumer magazines.

As any ad's designer, the better you understand these nuances, the better you will please your clients.

In creating your magazine ad you will make use of the following tools and techniques:

✔ Adjustment layers

✔ Free Transform

✔ Selection tools, Lasso and Marquee

✔ Layer masks

✔ Pen tool

✔ Paths

In addition to the specifics of ad creation, there are some Photoshop basics that will affect everything you do in the process. Be sure you understand the information in **Photoshop Essential 2.1** concerning dimensions, color modes, and resolution before diving in. Photoshop Essentials are located at the end of the project.

FIGURE 2-1

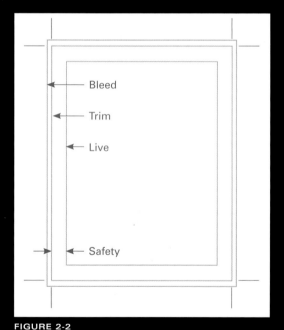

Bleed

Trim

Live

Safety

FIGURE 2-2

Using ad specs to set up your document

If you are new to print advertising, read the sidebar **Ad Specifications** before beginning this project.

This ad will be built to the mechanical specifications of a full page bleed ad for *The Hollywood Reporter.* Bleed, 8.625″ x 11.25″; Trim, 8.375″ x 11″; Live, 7.875″ x 10.5″ (.25″ from trim). The main sizes you need to worry about are bleed, the overall size of the document; and live, the area within which you need to keep all vital images and information. Usually, the Photoshop file is placed in a page layout program such as Adobe InDesign, Adobe Illustrator, or QuarkXpress, which allow you to create crop marks and add a legend with publication information, ad specs, and issue date. Also, type that does not need special effects is usually set in the page layout program rather than Photoshop. Always check the specs to see which file formats the publication accepts. Many pubs won't accept InDesign or Illustrator files, but will accept Quark files. Increasingly, the format of choice is Portable Document File (PDF). InDesign and Illustrator files can both be exported in PDF format.

1. Make a new Photoshop document 8.625″ x 11.25″. Normally, you would specify 300ppi for the resolution, the standard setting for high resolution final art, but to keep file size down for readers with smaller computers, this project will be built at half resolution, 150ppi. You may find, if you check the image size later, that the dimensions have changed to 8.627″ x 11.253″. This is probably because Photoshop requires documents to have an integral number of pixels. Don't worry about it—this variation is not enough to be significant. Choose 8 bit for the depth and CMYK for the color mode (**FIGURE 2-1**). Save the document, naming it Project2.psd.

AD SPECIFICATIONS

One of the first questions to ask when starting a print job is *what are the print specifications or ad specs?* These may also be referred to as the *mechanical specifications*. The specs are provided by the publication and contain detailed information about the dimensions and resolution requirements of the mechanical (the final artwork for the ad). Do not start the job until you have this information and, if possible, get a printout of the specs from the publication or printer. The media buy for the ad campaign will likely include two or more publications. You need to create your ad for the largest publication first, then resize and tweak it for the others. Occasionally, you can design an ad that will work for multiple publications if they are very close in size. All major publications now provide this information on their websites. It is sometimes referred to as an *online media kit*. Look for something that says Ad or Media Info. For example to get the specs for *The Hollywood Reporter*, go to thehollywoodreporter.com and click Ad Info in the navigation bar at the top of the page. Scroll down to Print Ad Info and click the link that takes you to the download page. Then, download THR Mechanical Ad Specifications.pdf. This will give you the sizes of all the various ad configurations.

There are a few terms with which you need to be familiar: Bleed, Trim, Live, and Safety. *Trim* is the actual final size of the magazine. The ad you are creating in this project will be a *full bleed* ad. That means the image will be printed right up to the edge of the page on all sides. To insure that no white paper shows in the event that the trimming of the magazine isn't perfect, you are required to build your image slightly larger than the actual trim size of the magazine. This is called the *bleed* size. Usually the bleed is about ⅛ inch on all sides. Think of this as the outside sloppiness factor. The inside

sloppiness factor is called *Live*. Live is the area within which all important information and images must be kept for the magazine to guarantee nothing vital will be lost during the trimming process. This is usually about ¼ inch, but can be as much as ½ inch. The distance between trim and live is called *safety* (**FIGURE 2-2**).

Unfortunately, publications have not standardized the way this information is presented on their spec sheets. Newer publications tend to list it as I have done here: bleed, trim, live; and they will convert the fractions to decimals. Older magazines make you work harder. For example, to find the size of a full page bleed ad in *The Hollywood Reporter*, you look under the section Bleed. There you will find the Full Page (untrimmed) size, that is the *bleed* size. Then they list the Full Page (trimmed) size, that is the *trim* size. They don't even list the live area. Rather, right under the Bleed heading it says keep all live matter ¼˝ from trim. So, to determine the live area, you have to subtract ½˝ (¼˝ each side) from the width and the height of the trim size. And, even though they require digital files (which means they have to be produced on the computer), they list everything in fractions rather than decimals. You have to convert the measurements to decimals in order to work with these sizes on your computer, which greatly increases the chance of error. I have found it helps to print the specs page and then use a highlighter to mark the information that concerns me. This process helps to focus on and clarify what the specs really are.

*Note: **Print** specifications are always listed width first, then height. For some reason, which I have yet to discover, **outdoor** specifications (billboards, bus sides, etc.) are always listed height first, followed by width.* ∎

FIGURE 2-3

2. To quickly establish the live area, make another new document 7.875"x 10.5". This will be a reference layer. Make the background color something other than white.

➤ Drag this layer into Project2.psd using the Move tool. Hold down the shift key as you do this and it will place the layer in the center of the document (**FIGURE 2-3**). This is a reference layer only.

➤ Turn on the Snap feature, View > Snap. Usually I find this feature annoying and leave it off, but this is one time when it is very useful. Drag a guide to the top, bottom, and each side of the reference layer. To place guides, reveal the rulers, Command-R/Ctrl-R. Click the top ruler and drag to place horizontal guides, click on the side ruler and drag for vertical guides. Once the live area is defined by the guides, delete the reference layer by dragging it to the trash icon located at the bottom of the Layers palette. You could also use the View > New Guide command. You'd put vertical guides at .375" and 8.25" and horizontal guides at .375" and 10.875". This does require some minor math. I find the first technique to be quick and, with the Snap feature's help, quite accurate.

➤ Save the document. The document you made to use as a live area reference can be closed without saving.

Tip: Press Command-; /Ctrl-; (semicolon) to show or hide the guides.

Before you actually begin building this ad, spend some time thinking about its purpose (how is this ad going to generate revenue and to whom is it speaking), what elements absolutely have to be in the ad, and what assets you have to work with. This is a trade ad intended to tell people who develop advertising media plans that this show delivers a lot of viewers. These viewers belong to a particular economic and education level with well-defined spending habits. The ad needs to reinforce the show's *brand*, reminding advertisers that this is the type of show with which they want their

COMPOSITING IMAGES

Assembling images seamlessly and harmoniously is largely what Photoshop is about. This process is often referred to as *compositing*. There are two main types of composites, realistic and montage. *Realistic* composites attempt to combine images in such a way that the final image doesn't look like a composite at all. Rather, it appears that all of the elements actually existed in the same space and time at the moment the photo was taken. *Montage* composites, on the other hand, combine images in an interesting way but with no attempt to make the final results look like a scene from real life. In this project you will create a montage composite. A big part of creating a successful composite, either realistic or montage, is choosing the right images. Here are a few important things to keep in mind when choosing your images.

1. **Camera angle:** Photoshop is not a 3D program. You can use a number of techniques to create the illusion of 3D, but, unless the object is completely flat to begin with (type, for example), you can't change the camera angle in any believable way. This is extremely important to consider when creating a realistic composite. If you have a photograph of a car from the side, for example, there is no way you can rotate the camera and look at that car from above. You would need a 3D modeling program to do that. Nothing makes a realistic composite look less realistic than mixing images of differing camera angles.

2. **Light source:** Light defines the three-dimensional space in which we live. A consistent light source and corresponding shadows are critical to a realistic composite. This is not essential in a montage, but even in this case, having a consistent or nearly consistent light source for the most important elements will help unify the final image. The montage you create in this project will not have a consistent light source in the background because the same image has been used multiple times and has been flipped horizontally, but the most important images, those of the talent, have the same or nearly the same light source. This helps unite them visually even though they clearly are not intended to look as though they were all photographed at the same time sitting together in the studio.

3. **Resolution and size:** To maintain the quality of an image, it is important to avoid scaling images up if at all possible. Therefore, you want start with images that are at or greater than the final size and resolution at which they will be used in the composite. If you were making an 8.5″ x 11″ ad for a high-end magazine and using a single image that fills the page, the scan of that image should be at least 8.5″ x 11″ at 300ppi (more will be said about resolution later in this project).

4. **Copyright:** If you haven't shot the photo yourself, someone else owns the copyright for that image. That means you cannot use that image without their permission. If there are people in the image, you need to be sure they have signed model releases. Not being an attorney, I can't give legal advice and copyright law can be very tricky. But experience has taught me that it needs to be taken very seriously. There are numerous websites devoted to this subject. Some of them contain interesting stories that dramatically illustrate the consequences of being ignorant of or ignoring copyright laws. ∎

products associated. Elements that must be included in the ad are the talent (news team); the headline; the show logo; and the tune-in information, which includes day, air time, and the network or station logo. It needs to feel big, and have plenty of production value. The only assets you have been given are images of the talent, the show logo, and network logo. All other images must be found in stock photography or shot by you or your photographer. As you look for images, think about how you will tell the story of this show. The show deals with the various issues of contemporary urban life: current events, politics, financial matters, health issues, etc. The challenge of a print ad is to tell the story in a single compelling frame. If this were an on-air spot, the story could be told over time, with many frames of motion, music, and voice-overs.

INFORMATION HIERARCHY AND VISUAL TRACKING

To be successful, an ad needs to be organized and designed in a way that will direct the reader's attention to the most important information first, then to the next most important, and so on. This is called the *Information Hierarchy*. In its most basic form this means the headline is at the top, followed by a subhead, then body copy, logo and tune-in at the bottom. You could think in terms of *what, where, when*. Yes, rules are made to be broken, but you need to know the rules first and the thinking behind them before you can break them successfully. The point is, if everything in the ad places the same demands on the reader's attention, the reader won't know where to look first and the ad will start to fall apart.

Visual tracking supports the information hierarchy by making sure the reader makes the right connections. Often a headline will make a statement, followed by a payoff line. In our ad for this project the headline makes the bold statement "The Most Watched Weekly News Magazine." To emphasize and qualify that statement is the one-word payoff "Ever" (period). If the payoff is too far away from the head, the two won't be visually connected and the reader won't "get it." You would then say the ad doesn't track. ■

Foundation: creating the background montage

Open the image **Buildings.tif** (**FIGURE 2-4**) from the Project Two folder; dismiss the Missing Profile dialog if it appears. This single image will be used to create the majority of the background montage. It has all the elements needed to create the look and feel the ad needs. The high-rise buildings relate to contemporary urban society; the classic columns can evoke the courts or financial institutions; the low angle adds a sense of drama. The only other image you will use in the background is the astrological globe. This element alludes to the show's title, *Our World*, and reinforces the global concept of the show. It will be treated in a highly graphic, stylized manner.

FIGURE 2-4

TRANSFORMATIONS

In this project, you will be doing a lot of scaling and rotating using the Transform command. Before you start, take time now to read **Photoshop Essential 2.2: The Free Transform Command**.

1. Make a group (*set* in CS) named BACKGROUND in your document Project2.psd. Then click Buildings.tif. Choose the Move tool and click either in the image window or in the Layers palette and drag the layer *Background* from Buildings.tif into your document Project2.psd. If the group BACKGROUND was highlighted and the arrow left of the group name is pointing down, the new layer should automatically become a member of that group. If not, drag it into the group. Rename the layer *buildings1* (**FIGURE 2-5**).

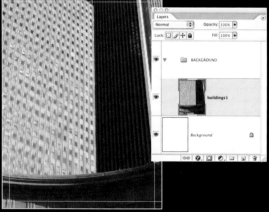

FIGURE 2-5

2. Duplicate layer *buildings1* **twice** by dragging the layer to the *New layer* button at the bottom of the Layers palette two times, or press Command-J/Ctrl-J twice. Name the duplicate layers *buildings2* and *buildings3* (**FIGURE 2-6**).

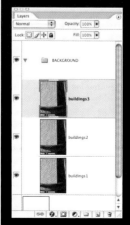

FIGURE 2-6

FIGURE 2-7

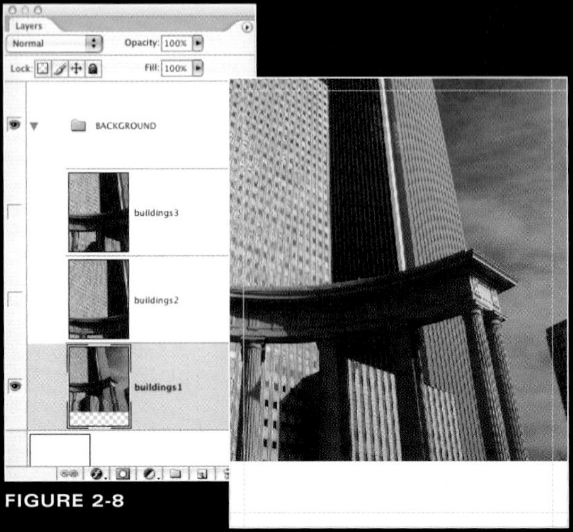

FIGURE 2-8

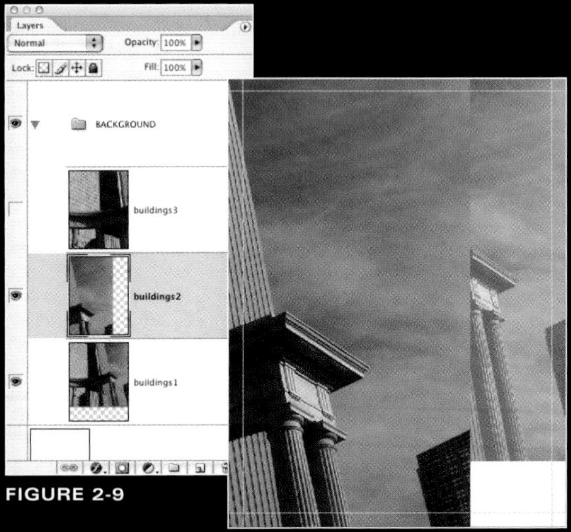

FIGURE 2-9

3. Hide layers *buildings2* and *buildings3*. With *buildings1* high-lighted, choose the Free Transform command (Command-T/Ctrl-T). Because the image is so large, the handles of the transform window may be out of view. To scale the image without using the handles, enter 54% in the Width field in the options bar (**FIGURE 2-7**). Click the chain symbol to link width and height to insure the image scales proportionately.

4. Drag the image up and to the right as shown in **FIGURE 2-8**. The exact position can be determined after you bring the talent into the composite. Click the check mark in the options bar or press Return/Enter to perform the transformation.

   ➤ Reduce the layer opacity to 69%.

Next, you will use layer masks to composite these images seamlessly. Read **Photoshop Essential 2.3: Layer Masks** at the end of the project.

Using layer masks to composite the background images

1. Show layer *buildings2*. Highlight the layer and with the Move tool, move the layer up and to the left so the high rise intersects the top left corner and the colonnade is just below center. (**FIGURE 2-9**).

2. Click the *Add layer mask* button at the bottom of the Layers palette to add a *reveal all* layer mask. The mask will be completely white and all of the image will be visible.

3. Select the Gradient tool and click the sample gradient at the left end of the options bar to open the Gradient Editor. In the Gradient Editor, choose **Foreground to Transparent** and click OK. Make sure your foreground color is black (press the D key). Choose Linear Gradient in the options bar. Start in the center of the image and drag at a downward angle toward the lower left side of the image. Try to make the line of the Gradient tool perpendicular to the lines of the high rise, and release at the edge of the high rise. The right side of the layer is masked, hiding

FIGURE 2-10

FIGURE 2-11

the sky on the right and revealing the building and colonnade on the left (**FIGURE 2-10**).

4. Make layer *buildings3* visible and highlight it. Choose the Free Transform command, Command-T/Ctrl-T, and then Control/Right-click to access the contextual menu. Choose Flip Horizontal from the contextual menu (**FIGURE 2-11**). Drag the image up and to the right so the end of the colonnade is about all you see.

> Rotate the image so the columns appear to be standing straight. Then scale the image by dragging the handle in the lower left of the Transform window up toward the upper right corner. Press Shift to constrain proportions; watch the scale percentage numbers in the options bar and stop at about 72%. Drag the image back in frame so the columns are positioned in the upper right corner of the document and click the check mark in the options bar or press Return/Enter to perform the transformation (**FIGURE 2-12**).

5. Hold down the Option/Alt key and click the *Add layer mask* button. This will add a *hide all* layer mask. The image disappears completely.

FIGURE 2-12

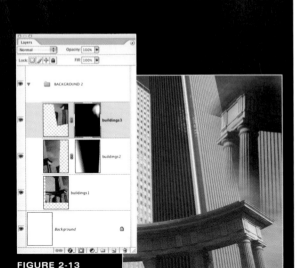

FIGURE 2-13

FIGURE 2-14

6. Choose a soft brush, about 200 pixels in diameter. Turn off Shape Dynamics in the Brushes palette (the Brushes and the Brushes palette are covered in depth in **Mini-Tutorial 1.1**). Make the foreground color white. Be sure you are working on the layer mask. Turn on the Airbrush and lower the flow to about 20%.

➤ Starting in the upper right corner, slowly start painting. As you paint, you will reveal the colonnade (**FIGURE 2-13**). If you reveal too much, press X to toggle the foreground/ background colors. Black is now the foreground color. Paint over the area you wish to conceal again. When I am fine-tuning a mask, I frequently toggle between black and white.

Tip: Sometimes when working on masks, the colors in the toolbox will end up being other than pure black and white. This is problematic, as you may think you have completely concealed part of an image only to find that it can be faintly seen when printed. That may be because the foreground color was a shade of gray rather than 100% black. It is also common to end up with both the foreground and background colors being white. You can return to the default settings of pure black and white by pressing D.

The Marquee and Lasso are great for making simple selections. In the next step you will use the Lasso to select a portion of the colonnade. **Photoshop Essential 2.4: Marquee and Lasso Tools** gives you detailed information on how these tools work.

Defining the edge of the colonnade to add strength and structure

A montage is stronger if some of the masked edges are well defined rather than soft blends. To define the edge of the colonnade in the upper right, use the Polygonal Lasso to make a selection around the upper left side. Zoom in close. Click at various spots along the structure to define the edge (**FIGURE 2-14**). Add a 2-pixel feather (Selection > Feather) and, with a 150-pixel soft brush, using white and a flow of about 30, paint along the left side of the selection. Make the upper left corner look solid, let the lower part fade into the background. To intensify the highlights and increase the overall contrast of this layer, change the blending mode to Hard Light. To make its presence even stronger, duplicate the layer by dragging it to the *New Layer* button at the bottom of the palette. Control the effect by reducing the layer opacity if necessary (**FIGURE 2-15**). Be sure to deselect and save your document.

Fill and adjustment layers

Fill and adjustment layers are critical to nondestructive image manipulation, especially for color and contrast correction. Stop now and read **Photoshop Essential 2.5: Fill and Adjustment Layers.**

In the next steps you will use a fill layer to make the images of the buildings monochromatic so as not to compete with the talent.

Tip: Limiting the color palette is one way to remove an image from the realm of everyday familiarity and make it more interesting. You will often see this technique used in ads and movie posters to make the image look more artsy, sophisticated, moody, or intriguing.

1. With *buildings2* highlighted, click the *Create New Fill or Adjustment Layer* button at the bottom of the Layers palette and add a *Solid Color* fill layer (**FIGURE 2-16**). When the Color Picker appears, choose a purple/gray color. Make a note of the CMYK percentages and click OK. Because this is a fill layer, no pixels are actually modified and the color can be easily changed later without degrading the image. At first, the images below are completely hidden by the fill layer.

    ➤ Change the Layer blending mode to Color. Now, the images show through, but they all have taken on the color of the fill layer (**FIGURE 2-17**).

2. The lower part of the image is where the logo and tune-in information for the television show will be placed. This information is critical to the ad. The reader must see and read it quickly. You will also be adding another graphic element, the astrological globe, in the lower left. To make sure that the buildings in the background don't compete with this information you are going to add a gradient that will hide much of the background in that area. You will create this gradient in two steps.

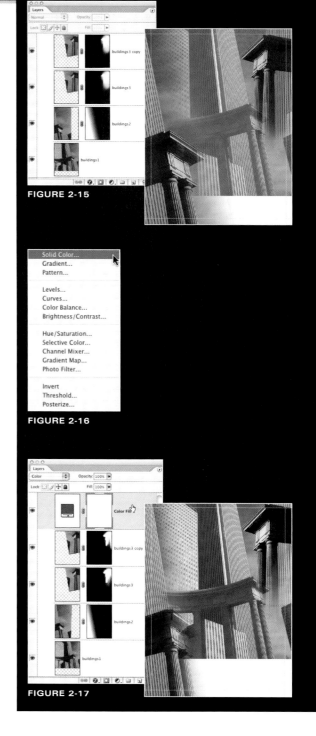

FIGURE 2-15

FIGURE 2-16

FIGURE 2-17

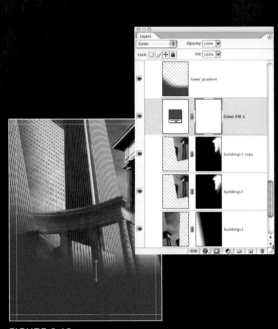

FIGURE 2-18

FIGURE 2-19

➤ Make a new layer above the color fill layer and name it *lower gradient*. Choose the Gradient tool. Be sure you have chosen Foreground to Transparent in the Gradient Editor. Make your foreground color a slightly darker shade of the color you chose for the color fill layer by opening the Color Picker, entering the CMYK percentages from the previous step and then choosing a darker value of that hue in the Color Field.

➤ Click at the bottom edge of *buildings1* (the bottom of the image on layer *buildings1*, not the edge of the image window) and drag up. Release the mouse button about ¾″ above the bottom, just high enough to completely conceal the edge of *buidings1*. On the same layer, make another drag from the lower left corner toward the center of the composition. This is where the globe will go (**FIGURE 2-18**).

Tip: It is important in a montage of this type that edges of the original scans are completely concealed, either by covering them with another layer, as in this case, or by using a layer mask. These edges may not be apparent on your monitor, but can show up when the piece is printed. Very unprofessional.

Using the astrological globe as a stylized graphic element

The astrological globe will be used behind the show title in a highly stylized, graphic way. The globe is a reference to the show title and the worldwide scope of the show's news coverage. It also adds a focal point, grounding the ad and drawing attention to the title.

1. Open the file **Globe.tif** (**FIGURE 2-19**). Often stock photos of objects or people shot against a white background such as this will include an *Alpha Channel* or a *Path* that will allow you to quickly make a selection of the object and, using a layer mask, hide or knock out the background. In **Mini-Tutorial 2: Creating paths with the Pen tool** at the end of this project you will learn

all about creating paths of your own. For now, click on the Paths palette to take advantage of the path created for you by the folks at PhotoSpin.com. Command/Ctrl-click *Clipping Path* in the Paths palette to turn the path into a selection.

2. Add a one-pixel feather, then click the *Add layer mask* button at the bottom of the Layers palette. Since there was an active selection when you added the mask, everything outside the selected area is concealed (**FIGURE 2-20**).

3. Drag the layer *globe* from Globe.tif into Project2.psd. Place it above *lower gradient* in the BACKGROUND group. As long as the link symbol appears between the layer and its mask, both the layer and the mask will be moved to the Project2 document (**FIGURE 2-21**).

4. Scale the layer to 87%. Position the globe so the inner zodiac band is just touching the guides for the live area (Command-; /Ctrl-; [semicolon] reveals guides). Change the layer blending mode to Color Dodge and reduce the layer opacity to 60% (**FIGURE 2-22**).

5. In this step you will modify the layer mask on the layer *globe*. Duplicate the layer first as a precaution by highlighting the layer and pressing Command-J/Ctrl-J. The reason for duplicating the layer is that you will be **modifying** the mask, and the clipping path you used to create the mask did not transfer to the final document with the layer, so you can't use it to reselect the globe if you need to. Remember, the background has not been eliminated, only hidden by the mask. By having a duplicate backup layer, you can easily return to the original mask if you mess up. The only reason I didn't have you apply the mask and erase the background is that I want you to get in the habit of working nondestructively. There will be many times when you will want to have the original background available. It's better to form the habit of keeping it rather than throwing it away. Rename the original globe layer *globe1* and the duplicate layer *globe2*. Hide *globe1*.

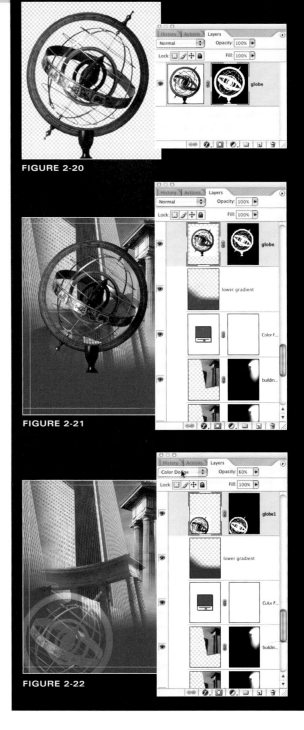

FIGURE 2-20

FIGURE 2-21

FIGURE 2-22

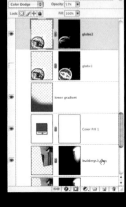

FIGURE 2-23

FIGURE 2-24

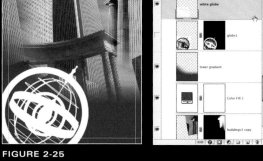

FIGURE 2-25

6. Working on the mask of *globe2* with a large soft airbrush (200 pixels in diameter), Shape Dynamics off and a flow of about 20%, black as the foreground color, start masking away the right side of the globe. You are going for an atmospheric effect with the upper left side of the globe being the most visible (**FIGURE 2-23**).

Tip: It will often be useful to see what the mask itself looks like. To view a layer's mask, Option/Alt-click on the mask in the Layers palette. **FIGURE 2-24** *shows you what the layer mask on* globe2 *looks like after the modifications have been made.*

7. Add a new layer below the layer *globe2*. Name it *white globe*. Command/Ctrl-click **on the layer mask** of *globe1* (the one which is currently turned off). Doing this will load the shape of the mask as a selection. Now fill the selection with white, Edit > Fill or, if your foreground color is white, Option-Delete/Alt-Backspace (**FIGURE 2-25**).

8. Deselect (Command-D/Ctrl-D). Add a *hide all* layer mask. Use a 200-pixel soft brush and white paint to gradually reveal the left portion of *white globe*. The point is to give the globe a more defined shape on the left side. This layer has no background so, as you reveal the layer, you see only the white shape of the globe (**FIGURE 2-26**).

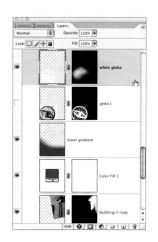

FIGURE 2-26

Construction:
adding the talent and the type

In this part of the project you will use the Pen tool to create paths around the talent, turn the paths into selections, and use the selections to knock out the backgrounds. Then you will bring each of them into the final document and blend or composite them into the background you have created. The Pen tool has become one of my favorites for making selections. It wasn't always so. At first I found this tool completely nonintuitive and awkward. But for making selections, it gives you far more control than any of the other selection tools we have looked at thus far. If you are new to the Pen tool or have been avoiding it, stop now and do **Mini-Tutorial 2: Creating paths with the Pen tool** at the end of this project.

After you have brought the talent into the ad, you will bring in the type and add the finishing touches. In Project 3 you will learn how to use the Type tool. For this project you have been provided with a separate file, **P2_Type_Logos.psd**, that contains all the type and logos you will need to complete the ad.

Tip: As your file gains more groups and layers it will be convenient to use this keyboard shortcut to get to a specific group or layer. If you are in the Move tool, Control/Right-click on the element you wish to edit. A contextual menu will show you all the groups and layers with visible pixels at that specific point in your document. If you are in any other tool press Command/Ctrl at the same time to access the Move tool. If you have named your groups in all upper case and your layers in lower case, you will be able to find what you are looking for very quickly. A word of caution: In CS, groups (called sets) inside groups and the layers within them will not show up. This has been fixed in CS2.

WORKING WITH CELEBRITIES' IMAGES

Actors, news anchors, and celebrities of all types are themselves products. Their success is largely dependent on public perception. They and their agents want to have as much control as possible over how they are portrayed in the media. Of course, they can't control every aspect of the media, but they can control to a large extent how they appear in advertising. The better known the celebrity, the more power they are likely to have over how their image will be used. Many times they will have *kill rights* or the right of *final approval.* Kill rights mean that they get to choose what images of themselves can be used for promotional purposes. If there is a photo they don't like, they can kill it, which means it can't be used under any circumstances. Final approval means they personally get to approve any ad in which they are featured before it can go to the publication. This is something you want to know up front because it may affect the way you approach the ad.

Here are some things you will want to keep in mind.

Many times because of design or lighting considerations you will want to flip an image. That is, rotate the image horizontally creating a mirrored version of the original. In general, avoid flipping the talent's image. And NEVER flip their image if they have final approval. Keep in mind these people have looked at hundreds, perhaps thousands of images of themselves. They have studied and analyzed them. And they have come to certain conclusions about how they photograph best. Many will only allow themselves to be photographed from a particular side or angle and may even have this specified in their contracts. You may not think they look any different when flipped, but you will be hard pressed to convince them of that. If you feel you absolutely must flip their image for some reason, you have to get permission to do so from them or their agent beforehand. If they do not have final approval, you may be able to get away with it, but always let your creative director or design director know that you have flipped the image and get their approval.

Be aware of contract considerations. I once did an ad for *Sixty Minutes II*, similar to the ad you are creating in this project. It had the talent featured against a montage background. The talent consisted of Dan Rather, Vicki Mabry, Bob Simon, and Charlie Rose. Originally, I designed the ad with Vicki Mabry in front. I just thought it looked better that way. Then, because I wanted to create the illusion of depth, the other members of the team became progressively smaller as if receding in space. The difference in size was very slight. However, this version was rejected because, so I was told, Dan Rather's image always had to appear larger than the other cast members when it appeared in print ads. If I kept the arrangement as it was and simply made him larger, then Vicki Mabry would appear dwarfed. I had no choice but to move Dan to the foreground. ■

KNOCKING OUT THE TALENTS' BACKGROUNDS

1. Open the image **Vince.tif**. Double-click the *Background* to open the New Layer dialog and convert it into a layer. Give it the name *vince*. Select the Pen tool. Be sure to choose **Paths** in the options bar (**FIGURE 2-27**). The default drawing option, Shape Layers, will be discussed in the next project. Create a path around Vince. It's important to zoom in close when using the Pen tool in order to make an accurate path. Try to make the path slightly inside the edge of the body. That way when you add a feather you won't pick up any of the background (**FIGURE 2-28**). Use fewer points where there is less detail (along the shoulders) and more points where there is greater detail (the hair).

2. When you have completed the path around Vince, Command/Ctrl-click the path thumbnail in the Paths palette. This will *load* the path as a selection. Add a 2-pixel feather and then add a layer mask (**FIGURE 2-29**).

3. Use the same steps to knock out the backgrounds on Lisa and Matt.

COMPOSITING THE TALENT IN THE FINAL DOCUMENT

If this were a real ad, these would be well-known celebrities, whose images would help sell the show. You need to be sure you present them in the best way possible. This means being careful to maintain the integrity of the images as you composite them. The main thing to avoid is having their heads blend too much into the background. It is important to keep their heads 100% opaque, except for the 2-pixel feather around the edge. Their bodies, however, do need to fade into the background in order to give the ad a unified appearance.

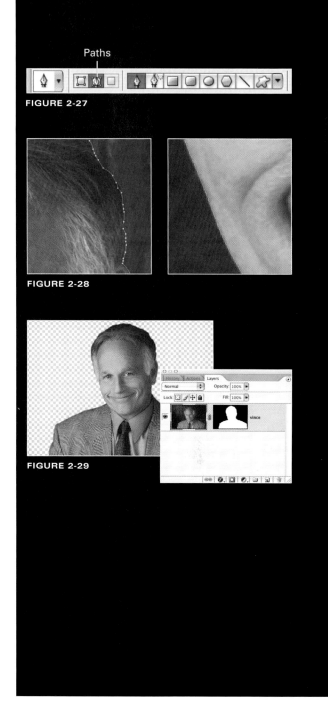

Paths

FIGURE 2-27

FIGURE 2-28

FIGURE 2-29

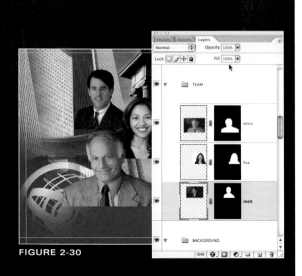

FIGURE 2-30

FIGURE 2-31

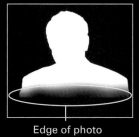

FIGURE 2-32   Edge of photo

1. Close BACKGROUND group and make a new group named TEAM. Drag the images of the talent into this new group. (Don't forget, if you leave group BACKGROUND open and make a new group, that new one will become a member of BACKGROUND, which is not what you want). Use Transform to scale each image and create some sense of three-dimensional space. Vince, the lead anchor, will be in the foreground and will be the largest. Lisa will be on the layer below him and will be a little smaller. Matt on the next layer will be smaller still (**FIGURE 2-30**). They should be arranged so as to communicate that this is a team, yet with enough space so as not to look crowded and to give them their own identities. When scaling the images, be sure to hold down the Shift key to constrain the images' proportions.

2. To blend the talent into the background, work with only one image at a time and use a large soft brush (about 200 pixels) with a low flow (about 20). Working from the bottom up, gradually mask away their bodies, blending them into the background (**FIGURE 2-31**). These images have been cropped so that there is very little chest area to work with. You need to be very careful to get just the right amount of fade before reaching the face. When you have finished, check the mask by pressing Option/Alt and clicking on the mask in the Layers palette. You want to be sure you have eliminated any hard edge along the bottom of the photo. You may need to choose a smaller brush, increase the flow, and paint right along the edge to make sure it is gone (**FIGURE 2-32**). Save your document.

ADDING THE TYPE AND LOGOS

Before you bring the type and logos into the ad, you need to create a place for them. These items all need to stand out from the background and be easily read. They also need to be integrated into the overall design—too often type looks as if it has just been stuck on top of an image. In this ad you will achieve both goals with the use of white gradient bands and strokes. These will tone down the background, creating a lighter area that will contrast with type and make an architectural structure that gives the type a place to live and holds the whole ad together.

1. Use the Polygon Lasso. Start at the upper left corner of the image and click. Move down the image staying parallel to the edge of the high rise. Click again below the center of the globe. Move right about 2.5 inches and click again. Move up to the top of the image and click about 5.5 inches to the right of where you began. Then click on the point where you began to close the path (**FIGURE 2-33**).

2. Add a 2-pixel feather. In the group BACKGROUND, make a new layer above *globe2* and name it *wht gradient*. Choose the Gradient tool. With white as the foreground color and **Foreground to Transparent** chosen in the Gradient Editor, click at the top of the image and drag down toward the globe. Release the mouse about two-thirds of the way down the image (**FIGURE 2-34**). To increase the effect, duplicate the layer. Reduce the opacity of the duplicated layer to 50%.

3. With the Rectangular Marquee tool, make a selection across the lower part of the page about 1.5 inches high. Make a new layer, name it *horizontal band*, and fill it with white. Position the band so it crosses through the center of the globe and deselect (**FIGURE 2-35**).

Tip: Watch the info palette when making the horizontal selection. It will tell you the dimensions of the selection.

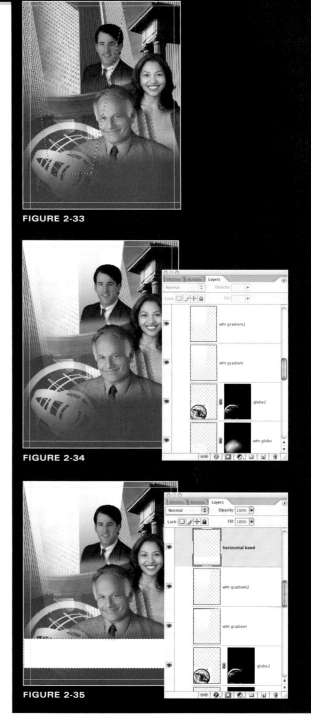

FIGURE 2-33

FIGURE 2-34

FIGURE 2-35

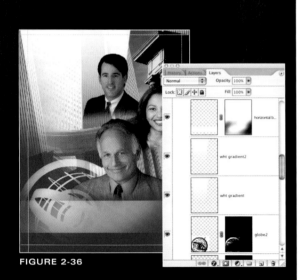

FIGURE 2-36

FIGURE 2-37

FIGURE 2-38

4. Add a Reveal All layer mask. With a 400-pixel soft brush (Shape Dynamics off), Airbrush on and a flow of about 10%, use black and gently mask the left and right sides of the white band. The show logo will be quite large and placed to the left of center in this band (refer to the image of the finished project at the beginning of this chapter). Keep this in mind as you mask, leaving the area where the logo will go more or less opaque. Reduce the layer opacity to 63% (**FIGURE 2-36**).

5. To anchor the tune-in information and add a linear design element, Command/Ctrl-click on the layer *horizontal band* in the Layers palette. Make a new layer and name it *stroke.* Choose Edit > Stroke and enter 2 pixels. This will give you a 2-pixel-wide outline of the layer *horizontal band*. You will use only the bottom part of this box (**FIGURE 2-37**). Add a layer mask. Leaving only the bottom segment of the box, mask the top segment and the two side segments. Then, still working on the mask, use a brush to paint the left and right ends of the remaining bottom segment so it fades or blends into the background. The effect is of a line emerging out of the background, becoming solid and then disappearing again into the background. Making the mask asymmetrical will be more interesting and less expected than if it were exactly the same on both ends. Try a longer, more gradual fade on the left and a short, more abrupt fade on the right (**FIGURE 2-38**).

6. Open the file **P2_Type_Logos.psd.** Close the group BACKGROUND and make a new group named TYPE/LOGOS at the top of the layer stack in Project2.psd. Drag the layers *headline, body copy, show logo, talent names, and tune-in* from P2_Type_Logos.psd into the new group and position them as shown in **FIGURE 2-39**. The guides you set for the live area will help to make sure the tune-in and logo stay inside it.

7. Center the show logo top to bottom within the horizontal white band. Place a guide at the bottom of the show logo and turn on Snap to Guides (View > Snap To > Guides), align the tune-in information with the bottom of the logo and move *stroke* up to align with the bottom of the logo and the tune-in. Look for ways to line things up, such as the body copy lining up with the E in *Ever* or the source line lining up with the bottom of the W in *World*. Small details like this make a big difference in the professional appearance of the ad.

FINISHING TOUCHES

OK, now look at the ad. Where are there problems? Is there anything you would like to enhance or change? The first I notice are legibility problems. The body copy and the talents' names are hard to read. Also, I think the ad could be a little more dramatic overall.

All of these can be solved with additional layers and some paint.

1. In the BACKGROUND group add a layer above *stroke* named *body copy glo*. Use the Lasso to make a selection around all the type, including the headline (**FIGURE 2-40**). Fill the selection with white. Deselect and blur the layer by going to Filter > Blur > Gaussian. Try a blur of about 20. Then lower the opacity of the layer to 70%.

2. Dark around the edges is always a good way to add drama and focus attention on the inside. Add a new layer above *lower gradient* and name it something like *dark border*. Use a very large soft airbrush, about 400 pixels, and sample one of the darkest colors in the image (Option/Alt while in the Brush tool will give you the eyedropper). Then, paint a circular border on the bottom and up the left side (**FIGURE 2-41**).

3. To make the talents' names more legible, add a layer above *body copy glo*. Make a new layer named *names glo*. The purpose of glows is usually to separate an element from the background. To do this you will often use a dark glow. Use the dark

FIGURE 2-39

FIGURE 2-40

FIGURE 2-41

FIGURE 2-42

FIGURE 2-43

color from the previous step, a brush of about 100 pixels and flow of about 10%. Slowly paint behind the names until they are more legible. Use a layer mask to clean up and refine these dark patches (**FIGURE 2-42**). Try to make the shapes irregular so they will look less mechanical and more like part of the background.

4. Finally, to make the talent stand out more and add yet a little more drama, create subtle glows behind the talent. Add one more layer, *talent glos*, and with white, gently paint glows over the shoulders of each of the talent (**FIGURE 2-43**). Save your document.

Getting rid of the excess

Click on layer *buildings2* and, with the Move tool chosen, check Show Transform Controls (in CS, Show Bounding Box) in the options bar. That will show you how much extra image is hanging out beyond the viewable image area (**FIGURE 2-44**).

All that extra image is eating up memory and increasing the file size. If you plan to send this file to a publisher or prepress house, it would be best to crop the document and get rid of the excess. Choose the Cropping tool, start at one corner, drag diagonally to the other so the entire image is selected, and press Return/Enter (**FIGURE 2-45**). When the crop is finished you will notice a considerable difference in the size of the document. Do a Save As; chances are there will be changes and you may need that excess later

Marketing and advertising is always about generating revenue in some way. Understand how that works in a particular case and you will have an insight into who the audience is and the angle you should take on the story. Every ad, brochure, commercial, and website tells a story. You have to know to whom you are speaking and why, then you know what story to tell. This is not peculiar to entertainment, but applies to all types of advertising.

WRAPPING UP

This project has been packed with tools and techniques that will be invaluable to you from now on. Nearly every professional Photoshop job you do will put these skills to use.

In the next project, you will learn about channels and how to use them to make complex selections quickly and to create interesting graphic effects. Also, you will learn how to use Photoshop's vector-based Type tool, Shape layers, and the amazing Layer Styles.

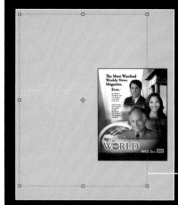

Transform Controls

FIGURE 2-44

FIGURE 2-45

When you create a new document, you must specify dimensions, color mode, resolution, and bit depth (**PE 2.1A**). These are big topics. It isn't necessary at this point to cover them in great detail, but you do need to understand a few of the basics.

Color Modes

On-air and web images need to be created in **RGB**—red, green, and blue. It is the native environment of computer monitors and television sets. In RGB, color is created by mixing light. The presence of all color makes white, the absence of all color makes black. This is the opposite of what you learned about mixing colors in elementary school. There, you were working with pigments, which produce color by reflecting light rather than mixing it. Pigments operate in the world of **CMY**—cyan, magenta, and yellow. With pigments the absence of all color is white (or the color of the paper) and the presence of all color (CMY) is black—in theory,

anyway. The presence of cyan, magenta, and yellow in equal amounts doesn't really produce black, but rather a muddy brown. Black pigment needs to be added to achieve true black, hence the *K* (black) in CMYK. K is used to represent black because B could be confused with blue in the RGB color mode. Images created for print will ultimately have to be reproduced in the CMYK color mode.

The goal of both color modes is to represent as closely as possible the colors we see in nature. Neither color mode, however, can reproduce the entire range of colors our eyes can see. Each has limitations. These limitations are referred to as the *gamut* of the color mode: the reproducible range of color. RGB is capable of reproducing far more colors than CMYK. Thus, it is said to have a wider gamut. If you are creating an image for print, it is very important to be aware of this. The RGB images seen on your monitor are *always* more vivid and colorful than the same images reproduced on a press in CMYK. That said, Photoshop does give you the option of working in RGB, but viewing the image as it will appear in CMYK.

There is an ongoing debate over whether images intended for print should be created from the outset in CMYK or if they should be created in RGB and later converted to CMYK. The pros of working in RGB are wider gamut and smaller file size. Because RGB can reproduce a wider range of colors, you have more information to work with, and it could be argued that having more information will give you better results. An RGB file will be much

PE 2.1A

smaller than a CMYK file with the same number of layers, masks, etc. The reason lies in the Channels, which will be discussed in detail in the next project. In brief, channels store the color information for your document, one channel for each color. That means three color channels for RGB and four channels for CMYK. That one extra channel may not seem like much until you consider the fact that information for every layer, adjustment layer, layer style, shape layer, layer mask, vector mask, and so on has to be kept in memory for that extra channel. This can make the file size of a CMYK document much, much larger.

But there is one drawback to working in RGB and it's a big one. Before your document can be printed it must be converted to CMYK. However, many features, such as adjustment layers, can't be converted from one color mode to another. This is not a big deal if you intend to provide only a *flattened* version of the document to the printer. A flattened document is one in which all of the layers have been merged. You can do a *save as* and save it as a flattened (no layers) tiff or eps. Open that document, convert it to CMYK, fine-tune the colors, and you're good to go. But, these days, most people I know also like to provide the pub or prepress house with a layered version of the file. This is true for any advertising, but it is especially true in entertainment where you are usually working against tough deadlines and by the time your files are delivered you are nearly out of time. If corrections or changes are needed, there may not be time for you to make them and send a new file. Or there may be changes related to ink density or spot colors that only the prepress house is qualified to make. In these cases, it's not unusual to have the prepress house make the changes and email you a jpeg for approval. To do that they must have the layered file. For this reason I have come to the conclusion that if an image is intended to be printed in CMYK, it is best to create the original document in CMYK. If file size becomes an issue, there are steps you can take to deal with that. Images intended for on-air or web should be created in RGB.

Dimensions and Resolution

As with color mode, you need to know how your final image will be used to determine the dimensions and resolution. If the image will be printed, you need to specify dimensions in terms of inches, centimeters, or millimeters, and resolution in pixels per inch. For a document to look good when printed it must be created at a much higher resolution than a document intended for on-air or web. Dimensions and resolution are inseparably linked, and both must be considered when creating the original document. The resolution of magazines and newspapers is specified in *lines per inch*. When creating a print file the rule of thumb is to set the Photoshop document's resolution at double the publication's number of lines per inch, and the dimensions 100% of the final size. Since most magazines are printed at 150 lines per inch or less, if you use 150 lines per inch as your standard you should be OK. Thus, if the trim size of the magazine is 8.5″ x 11″ you would make your document 8.5″ x 11″ at 300ppi.

To help you understand the relationship between dimension and resolution, take a moment now and make a document 5″ x 10″, RGB at 100ppi. After the document has opened, go to Image > Image

continues…

Size. Be sure the box at the bottom, *Resample Image*, is *not* checked (**PE 2.1B**). Now, increase the resolution to 200ppi. Notice the dimensions are cut in half, but the file size (shown at the top of the dialog) remains the same. Every time you change either the dimensions or the resolution the other will also change, but the file size remains the same. This is because you are taking the same number of pixels and either spreading them out over a larger area or condensing them into a smaller area. Owners of digital cameras are probably familiar with this phenomenon. When you take a high resolution photograph and open it in Photoshop, the resolution may be 72ppi but the physical dimensions are huge. To fix this, open Image Size and, with Resample Image **off**, change the resolution to 300ppi and the dimensions will be reduced to a more manageable size. The overall file size in megabytes will remain the same.

Resample Image actually changes the number of pixels in the image. If you increase either the dimensions or the resolution, pixels will be added and the file size will be increased. Decrease either dimensions or resolution and pixels are discarded and the file size will be reduced.

Bit Depth

Bit depth, also referred to as pixel or color depth, measures how much color information is available for displaying or printing each pixel. The greater the bit depth, the greater the amount of color information available; thus, the more accurate the color representation. In the New dialog you can specify 8 or 16 bit. Currently, most of the images you work with, including all of the images in this book, will be 8-bit. No doubt, this will change in the near future, with more and more images being created in 16-bit. CS2 has been developed with that in mind. Most of its tools and features will work with 16-bit images.

Be sure this box
is not checked.

PE 2.1B

Transform is Photoshop's term for changes in scale, rotation, and/or proportion. If you want to flip or rotate the entire document, you go to Image > Rotate Canvas and choose from the options available in the submenu. If you want to limit the transformation to specific objects or layers, you need to use the Transform command reached from Edit > Transform. The Transform commands fall into two types: presets that allow you to perform specific transformations, such as rotate, scale, skew, etc.; and the Free Transform command.

The Free Transform command (Edit > Free Transform or Command-T/Ctrl-T) allows you to perform multiple operations in a single move. You can scale, rotate, move, and distort all at the same time. Transformations are destructive and they do tend to degrade the image. It is a good idea to do as much in a single move as possible, because the more individual transformations you apply to an image, the more the image will degrade. The one exception to this is making very large changes in scale. If you need to enlarge or reduce an object by more than 50%, you will get better results if you do it in stages. Avoid scaling an image down and then scaling it back up. Instead, use Command-Z/Ctrl-Z to undo the previous move, then scale it to the desired size.

When using any of the Transform commands, the area to be transformed will be surrounded by a marquee with eight square handles. While this marquee is active, you can zoom and navigate, but you can't perform any other operation. You must first perform the transformation by pressing Return/Enter or cancel it by pressing Esc. As long as the marquee is active, you can switch to any other Transform command on the fly: Ctrl/Right-click in the image window and choose a command from the contextual menu (**PE 2.2A**).

In CS and CS2 you can transform multiple layers by linking them. In CS2 you can simply highlight the layers you wish to transform in the Layers palette. As long as the layers are highlighted, they will act as though they are linked. In both CS and CS2 this only works as long as there isn't an active selection. If there is an active selection, the transformation will apply only to that selection.

When using the Free Transform command, you can scale an object by dragging one of the corner handles. To constrain the proportions of the object, hold down the Shift key as you drag. To scale from the center out, add Option/Alt as you drag. If you drag from a handle other than one of the corner handles, you will either condense or extend the image along a single axis. You can't constrain the aspect ratio when dragging one of these handles. To distort the object, Command/Ctrl-drag one of the

Free Transform Path

Scale
Rotate
Skew
Distort
Perspective
Warp

Rotate 180°
Rotate 90° CW
Rotate 90° CCW

Flip Horizontal
Flip Vertical

PE 2.2A

continues...

Reference point location

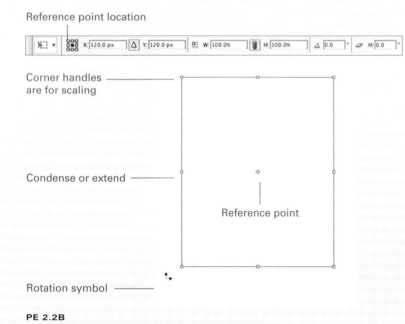

Corner handles
are for scaling

Condense or extend

Reference point

Rotation symbol

PE 2.2B

corner handles. This is useful for creating a sense of perspective. To rotate an object, choose the Free Transform command and move your pointer outside the marquee area. The pointer will turn into the rotate symbol. Drag in the direction you wish to rotate, and the object will rotate around the reference point. You can change the location of this point by dragging the point to a new location or by using the reference point location buttons in the options bar (**PE 2.2B**).

You can also make transformations numerically by entering the appropriate values in the options bar. Or, you can highlight the width or height fields in the options bar and use the arrows on your keyboard to enlarge or reduce the object incrementally. Click the link between width and height to scale proportionately. This technique is very helpful when you are working in close and can't get to the handles (**PE 2.2C**).

Set horizontal and vertical scale

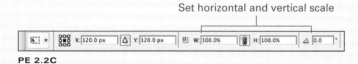

PE 2.2C

Layer masks allow you to composite images seamlessly and nondestructively. To add a mask to a layer click the *Add Layer Mask* button at the bottom of the Layers palette or go to Layer > Reveal All. If no selection is active at the time you add the mask, you will get a mask that *reveals all* (**PE 2.3A**). It is completely white. If you hold down Option/Alt and click the *Add Layer Mask* button, you will get a mask that conceals all. It is completely black and everything on the layer disappears (**PE 2.3B**). If you have an active selection (in this

case, we selected the car) and you add a mask, the selected area will appear white on the mask and the area outside the selection will appear black. Thus, the selected area will be visible and the non-selected area will disappear (**PE 2.3C**). Hold down Option/Alt as you add the mask and the reverse happens (**PE 2.3D**). If, for some reason, you end up with the area you wanted to see being invisible and the area you wanted to hide being visible, click on the layer mask and press Command-I/Ctrl-I to *invert* the colors on the mask. The areas of white and black are reversed.

Be sure you are actually working on the mask and not on the image. In CS2 the mask thumbnail next to the layer name in the Layers palette will be framed when you are on the mask (**PE 2.3E**). In CS the mask symbol appears next to the layer name. Normally in CS, when you are working on the image,

Add layer mask button

PE 2.3A

PE 2.3B

PE 2.3C

PE 2.3D

PE 2.3E

continues...

the symbol of the paintbrush appears there. Pay attention to these indicators, because it is easy to make the mistake of thinking you are on the mask when you are really on the image. You can really mess up your image this way.

The only color options you have for working on the mask are black, white, and shades of gray. If you see any other colors at the bottom of the toolbox,

you know you are working on the image, not on the mask. It is usually best to work with pure black and pure white, especially if you are new to masking. Sometimes, unintentionally, you will get a situation where the colors are both white, both black, or one may be a shade of gray. If this happens, restore the colors to 100% black foreground and 100% white background, by pressing D (default). It is very helpful when fine-tuning your masks to switch back and forth between black and white. Press X to quickly toggle or (reverse) the foreground and background colors.

Notice the link between the layer and the mask. As long as that link is on, the mask and the layer will move together and scale together. Unlink them and they can be moved and scaled independently of one another (**PE 2.3F**).

Link area for image and mask

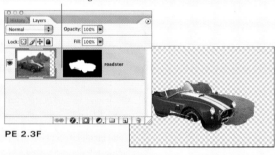

PE 2.3F

PE 2.3G

PE 2.3H

Sometimes it is useful to see what the mask itself looks like. To view only the mask, Option/Alt-click the mask in the Layers palette (**PE 2.3G**). Repeat the procedure to view your layers again. To deactivate a mask, Shift-click on the mask. A red X will appear over the mask, indicating that it is not currently active. Click the mask again to reactivate it (**PE 2.3H**).

Tip: When adding a layer mask it is usually wise to add a feather to the selection first. This will help the element blend with the layers below. No feather will often result in a cut-out look. The amount of feather is determined by the resolution of the document and how gradually you want the effect to fade. In general, for a high-res document (300ppi and above) 2 or 3 pixels is fine and for a low-res document, 1 or 2 is sufficient. Increase these numbers for a more gradual fade.

Marquee
Lasso

PE 2.4A

A **selection** is a defined area that you wish to either edit, protect, or mask. The selected area is indicated by a marquee—a moving broken line, commonly referred to as "marching ants." Two classes of tools used for making basic selections are the **Marquee** tools and the **Lasso** tools (**PE 2.4A**).

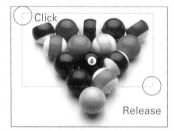
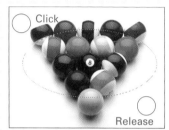

PE 2.4B

PE 2.4C

Click, Option/Alt drag   Click, Option/Alt drag

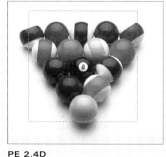

PE 2.4D

The **Marquee** tools have four varieties: Rectangular, Elliptical, Single Row, and Single Column. To use either the Rectangular or Elliptical Marquee tools, just drag across the image. The point where you click first becomes one corner of the selection and where you release becomes the opposite corner (**PE 2.4B**). Hold down Shift as you drag, to make a perfect square with the Rectangular marquee or a perfect circle with the Elliptical Marquee (**PE 2.4C**). Hold down Option/Alt to make a selection that expands equally in all directions, with your starting point as its center (**PE 2.4D**). The other two types of marquees are Single Row and Single Column. I haven't found much use for either one. One makes a selection that spans the width of the image, the other the height of the image; but the selections are both only one pixel wide.

In the options bar for the Marquee tools, use the selection options to choose how multiple selections in a single layer are treated (**PE 2.4E**). You can also specify a feather amount, apply anti-aliasing, and choose a style which determines the relationship between the height and width of the marquee. More about the selection options in a moment, but first a few words about feathering. You almost always want some feather on your selections. Usually, just one or two pixels is enough feather to soften the edge and make the selection look less cut-out. I prefer to add the feather after I make a selection by going to Select > Feather. If you specify a feather amount in the options bar, chances are

Selection options buttons

PE 2.4E

continues...

you will forget to change it back to zero and future selections will automatically be given a feather you didn't expect or want. When using the Elliptical Marquee, you can choose to apply anti-aliasing. This will add a row of pixels along the edge of the selection that blend with the surrounding area, creating the appearance of a smoother edge. (Anti-aliasing was discussed in detail in Project One). This option is not available for the Rectangular Marquee because when you are dealing with right angles, there is no need for anti-aliasing—the jagged edges only appear along curves or angles other than 90°.

PE 2.4F

PE 2.4G

PE 2.4H

Also in the options bar is the Style menu. *Normal* makes a selection without constraints, *fixed ratio* makes a selection that maintains a specified proportion, and *fixed size* makes a selection of a specified dimension. Use the Width and Height fields to specify the aspect ratio or the fixed size dimension.

There are three varieties of **Lasso** tools: the normal Lasso, which I like to think of as freeform; Polygonal; and Magnetic Lassos (**PE 2.4F**). As the name suggests, the freeform Lasso lets you make irregular selections by dragging, or *drawing*, around the area you wish to select. You have to be careful to finish drawing your selection by ending at the same point you began before you let go of the mouse or lift the stylus. If you release too soon, the path will automatically be closed by way of a straight line from where you released directly to where you started (**PE 2.4G**). This can be frustrating, and shortly I will tell you how to avoid it. With the Polygonal Lasso you click, release, move, and click (**PE 2.4H**). This creates a selection made up of straight lines connecting the points where you clicked. With this tool the path doesn't close until you click on the starting point, or press Return/Enter.

To avoid having the freeform Lasso close the path automatically when you release, hold down Option/ Alt. By holding down Option/Alt you can make either the freeform or Polygonal tool perform like the other. As long as Option/Alt is held down, the free-form Lasso won't automatically close and you can click, release, move, click to get straight segments if needed and then start dragging again to get free form segments; and the Polygonal Lasso can draw irregular selection segments.

The Magnetic Lasso tool works great in certain limited situations The rest of the time it is pretty much useless. To make a selection with this tool, click and draw around the area you wish to select. Unlike the Lasso, there's no need for you to make a careful selection—the tool will do the work for you. Points will be automatically placed along the way based on the tolerances you set in the options bar. This only works in areas of well-defined contrast.

Now, about the selection options: This is a feature you really need to become familiar with. It can be a great help or the source of major frustration. What you choose here affects the way your selections are constructed. For example, if you choose the first one (New Selection) and make a selection, then release and make another selection, the first selection disappears, leaving only the second one. If you choose the second option (Add to Selection), when you make a selection, release, and make another selection, both the first and the second selection remain active. You have added to the selection. The third choice subtracts the new selection from the existing selection (Subtract from Selection); and the fourth one makes a selection containing only the areas that intersect (Intersect With Selection). If your tool is ever acting unexpectedly, the first thing to do is check to see which option is chosen.

As long as you are using any of the selection tools and not the Move tool, the selection can be moved without affecting the image. If you are using the Move tool, you will actually cut the image and move the pixels.

A word of caution: Be careful not to confuse the Marquee tools with the Shape tools further down in the palette. I have often seen students become very frustrated because they are unable to make a rectangular selection, only to find they are using a Shape tool and not a Marquee tool.

Fill layers and adjustment layers are special kinds of layers. They do not contain pixels, but rather the fill or adjustment layer applies an effect to the layers below it. Fill and adjustment layers are totally nondestructive and they can be altered at any time. We will be discussing various fill and adjustment layers in detail in the projects ahead. This is a brief introduction to get you started. Fill layers let you apply a solid color, a gradient, or a pattern to the layers below. These layers will completely hide the layers below them unless used at a reduced opacity, with a blending mode other than Normal, or restricted by masking or group blending mode. Adjustment layers let you modify the characteristics, such as color or contrast, of the lower layers.

To add a fill or adjustment layer, click the half-black-half-white circle button at the bottom of the Layers palette (**PE 2.5**). Choose the type of fill or adjustment you want to use from the pop-up menu.

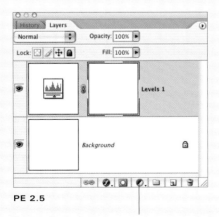

PE 2.5

Add fill or Adjustment layer

It is important to note that fill and adjustment layers affect *all* layers below them. There are times when this is very useful, as in this project when you want to make the background montage monochromatic. More often, though, you will want the effect of the fill or adjustment layer to apply only to the layer directly below. There are several ways to restrict the effect of an adjustment layer: masking using the layer mask, using the previous layer as a clipping mask, and changing the group blending mode.

Each fill and adjustment layer automatically comes with a mask, which behaves exactly like other layer masks. You can use them to restrict the area of the fill or adjustment layer. White will reveal the effect; black will conceal it.

You can also use the layer below the fill or adjustment layer as a clipping mask (Command-Option-G/Ctrl-Alt-G) to limit the area affected by the fill or adjustment layer. It will only affect the clipping mask layer. Another way to control the effect of an adjustment layer is with group blending modes. This technique doesn't work for the fill layers—Solid Color, Gradient, and Pattern. Groups have blending modes, just like layers do, but groups have one mode not available to layers. It is called *Pass Through* and it is the default mode for groups. As long as the group is using Pass Through mode the effects of the adjustment layers can "pass through" the group and affect everything below. If, however, the mode is changed to *Normal*, the effects of adjustment layers will be confined to layers within the group.

mini-tutorial 2

Creating paths with the Pen tool

The Pen tool is my favorite tool for making selections. It gives you the most control and flexibility, but it is one of the least intuitive of all the tools and can be very frustrating at first. To make a selection with the Pen tool you must first create a **path**. A path can be thought of two ways: as points connected by straight or curved segments, or as segments defined by points. All paths in Photoshop are Bézier curves, named for the engineer who invented the mathematical formulas that define them. Paths are vector based (resolution independent) and *they are completely independent of the layers in your Layers palette*.

Points are sometimes referred to as *anchor* points. Technically, all points on a path are anchor points, points at which the segments of the path are anchored. We will simply call them points. There are two types—corner points and smooth points. Corner points connect straight or sharply curved paths and smooth points connect curved segments. The latter come with two direction points connected to the anchor point by direction lines. The direction points and their direction lines are sometimes referred to as handles, and are used to manipulate curves.

THE TOOLS

The Pen tool submenu holds five variations of tools: Pen, Freeform Pen, Add Anchor Point, Delete Anchor Point, and Convert Point. The Pen tool works in combination with the Path Selection and Direct Selection tools. The Freeform Pen tool is too inaccurate to be of much use in most situations, so we won't spend any time on it.

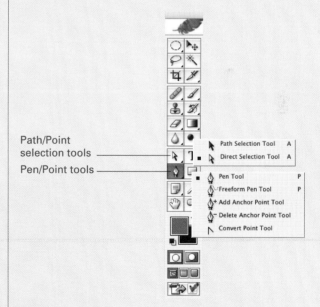

Path/Point selection tools

Pen/Point tools

Path Selection Tool   A
Direct Selection Tool   A

Pen Tool   P
Freeform Pen Tool   P
Add Anchor Point Tool
Delete Anchor Point Tool
Convert Point Tool

The Add Anchor Point and Delete Anchor Point tools work automatically when the Auto Add/Delete box is checked in the options bar.

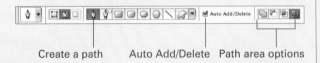

Create a path   Auto Add/Delete   Path area options

When you move the Pen over a portion of a path that has no point, it changes to the Add Anchor Point tool. If you click the path with it a point will be added. If you move the Pen over an existing point, it will become the Delete Anchor Point tool. Click and the point will be removed. The path you create appears in the Paths palette.

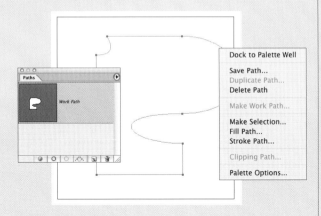

Using the Pen tool

1. Open the document **Grid.tif** from the Project Two folder on the CD. First you will create a simple triangle of straight segments. Choose the Pen tool. There is no need to add a new layer at this time because paths are independent of layers. Rather, keep an eye on the Paths palette. That is where your path lives. Click and release at the intersection of two grid lines. If you click and release without dragging, you get a corner point. If you click and drag, even a little bit, the point becomes a smooth point. The Shift key constrains the segments to perfectly horizontal, vertical, or 45° angles. Hold Shift, move to the left, and click at the next intersection. Move to the intersection directly below and click again. Then click on the starting point.

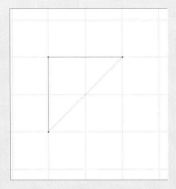

2. Now for a simple circle. In the Paths palette click in the area below the work path to deactivate it. The italicized words Work Path in the Paths palette are a clue that there is something special about that path. Work paths are volatile, meaning that they are not saved automatically and will disappear if the path is not highlighted in the Paths palette and another path is started. There's no need to save this first path, so click in a blank area of the Paths palette so the path is no longer highlighted. Then, to make a new path, click at an intersection, press Shift, and drag to the right, releasing when the end of the direction point touches the second line over. Move down three lines and click on the intersection directly below the first point and drag to

the left until the direction point touches the second line over. Then click on the starting point. Do not drag when you click on the starting point. If you were careful to click at the intersections and the direction points were exactly two columns wide, you should end up with a perfect circle.

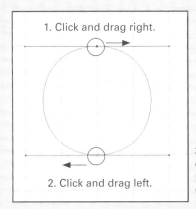

1. Click and drag right.

2. Click and drag left.

3. Close path by clicking on start point. Do not drag.

3. Compound curves are a little trickier. Click in a blank area of the Paths palette so the path you just created is no longer highlighted. Click again at an intersection on the grid and drag the left direction point out past the first line and about a third of the way into the next column and release. Go down two lines, click at the intersection directly below the starting point, and drag to the right‹about the same distance as before, but in the opposite direction. Notice that as you drag the direction point the curve changes. Every time you move one direction point it causes the other to move, too. This takes some getting used to and can be very frustrating to the novice. Move down two lines and click directly below the first point (now you¹re four lines down) and drag out to the left

the same distance as you did the first direction point. You now have two half circles of the same size facing opposite directions. To end the path and deselect all the points, Command/Ctrl-click away from the path.

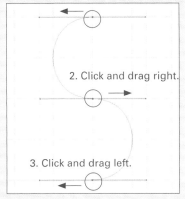

1. Click and drag left.

2. Click and drag right.

3. Click and drag left.

4. When creating a path around an object it is often necessary to change direction abruptly. To do this you need to get rid of the direction line that is leading you into the next curve. If you don't, you will get a weird little loop that is hard to eliminate. By pressing Option/Alt and clicking on the anchor point, you can kill that direction line and change directions. Deactivate the previous path and start a new one.

➤ Follow the same steps as previously, except after you pull the direction line on the second anchor point out to the right, Option/Alt-click on that anchor point. That eliminates the direction line. Now, drag in the opposite direction. The direction line you are dragging now is directly on top of the previous left direction line, so you can't see it. You know it is there because when you make the next anchor point, two lines down, and drag to the right, you get a nicely shaped half circle. If it weren't there, you would have to create the half circle with only the direction lines of the lower path point and that would be very tough.

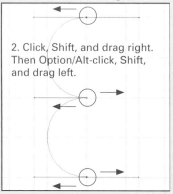

1. Click, Shift and drag left.

2. Click, Shift, and drag right. Then Option/Alt-click, Shift, and drag left.

3. Click, Shift, and drag right. Then Option/Alt-click, Shift, and drag left.

5. Another combination you will need is changing from a curve to a straight line. This one is easy. Make a half circle as in the previous step. Option/Alt-click on the second point *and don't drag*. This time move straight down and click again. As long as you don't drag you will get a perfectly straight segment. Another way to ensure a straight line is to hold the Shift key as you move downward to the next point. Not dragging is easy if you are using a mouse, but if you use a stylus, as I do, it is easy to drag just the slightest bit. Then you will have made a smooth point and not a corner point.

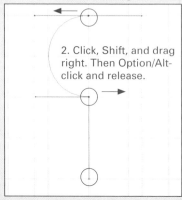

1. Click, Shift and drag left.

2. Click, Shift, and drag right. Then Option/Alt-click and release.

3. Click, do not drag

6. Now, combine these techniques. Start a new path, and refer to the figure shown here.

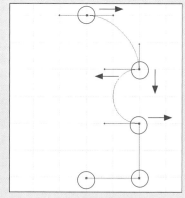

1. Click, Shift, and drag right.

2. Click, Shift, and drag down. Then Option/Alt-click and drag left.

3. Click, Shift, and drag right. Then Option/Alt-click and release.

4. Click, release.

5. Click, release.

➤ At point 1, click, Shift, and drag to the right, release at the first line.

➤ At point 2, click, Shift, drag down one row, then Option/Alt-click on the same point and drag to the left one and one-third columns.

➤ At point 3, click and drag to the right one and one-third columns, then Option/Alt click on point 3, eliminating the right direction point.

➤ Move to point 4 and click, do not drag. Move to point 5 and click. To end the path and deselect all the points, Command/Ctrl-click away from the path.

7. Choose the Path Selection tool (black arrow) and click on the path. This tool selects all the points at the same time. Copy and paste the path. It will be pasted directly on top of the original. Choose Edit > Free Transform Path (Command-T/Ctrl-T) and Control/Right-click in the transform area; choose Flip Horizontal from the contextual menu. Press Return/Enter to perform the transformation.

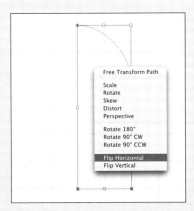

8. With the Path Selection tool still active and the duplicated path still selected, press Shift-left arrow key to move the path to the left. When the ends of the paths are close to overlapping, press the arrow key without Shift for finer control. Zoom in to the area where the top ends of

the paths come close to overlapping, as shown here. With the Pen tool, click the end point of one path, then the end point of the other. This will connect the paths with a small segment between the points. Do this for the points on the top and bottom, creating a closed path.

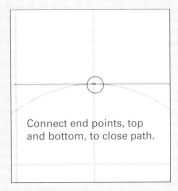

Connect end points, top and bottom, to close path.

➤ Save and name the path using the Path palette menu. To me this shape resembles a pepper mill, so I named mine *mill*. This path can now be turned into a selection or *loaded* as a selection by clicking on the Load Path as a Selection button at the bottom of the Paths palette. Better yet, Command/Ctrl-click on the path in the Paths palette to load the selection.

9. Make a new layer in the Layers palette, name it, and fill it with a color.

One other important tool you need when working with Paths is the Direct Selection tool—the white or open arrow tool. With it you can select and manipulate individual points. This is important when you want to fine-tune your path. Access the Direct Selection tool while in the Pen tool by holding down Command/Ctrl.

That's essentially all there is to it. All you need to do now is practice, practice, practice. As you do, here are a few things to keep in mind.

➤ The path area options buttons in the Pen tools options bar determine how compound paths are loaded as selections. If you get an unexpected result when you load a selection, check these buttons. More than likely, the wrong one is chosen.

➤ Use as many points as you need, but not more than you need, especially along curved segments. One reason for this is that each point can potentially cause a bump when loaded as a selection. If this happens, deactivate the selection, reactivate the path, and use the direction points of the anchor point causing the bump to correct the problem. This isn't always easy.

➤ Work up close and personal. If you plan to add a feather, make your path slightly inside the edge of the object to accommodate a feather and prevent a halo (the effect when part of the background is picked up by the feather).

➤ The path doesn't have to be perfect the first time. The beauty of paths is that you can go back and fine-tune them before loading one as a selection.

HART

ABANDONADO

music promo

Branding, genre, and design conventions

Key art is an important component of every advertising campaign. It is the graphic image that will be used throughout the
advertising campaign—in print ads, on billboards, bus sides,
kiosks, and so on. Key art can refer to a photographic image
only, sometimes called the hero. But, often it means the total
graphic package, including typography, logos, and design
elements.

3

3 music promo

When developing key art, it's helpful to keep in mind a few basic marketing concepts: branding, genre, and design conventions.

branding

Marketers seek to influence behavior by establishing in the mind of the consumer associations between their product and certain attributes. This is referred to as *branding*. It creates an *identity* and offers a *promise*—"this car is hot and if I drive it women will be attracted to me," or "this CD is romantic and it will set the mood." To be effective, branding must present a clear and consistent message.

genre

Artistic works of all kinds can be divided into categories based on form, style, subject matter, or marketing criteria. These categories are referred to as *genres*. The basic classifications are very broad and become narrower with many subgenres. Some of the broad classifications for movies and television are Comedy, Sitcom, Drama, Horror, Documentary, Mystery, and Historical. Among music's many classifications, some of the broad categories are Rock, R & B, Hip-Hop, Jazz, Classical, and Pop. Each of these has many subcategories or subgenres. Some promoters try to convince us that their artist or artists are in a genre all their own, in an attempt to differentiate them from other performers. Knowing the genre will often give you insights into the personality and mindset of the audience. This will be of great help when it comes to choosing images and fonts, and making design decisions of all kinds.

This project deals with a music genre. The next two projects will address genre as it applies to television and movies.

design conventions

Associated with each genre, whether in music, television, or movies, are certain images, colors, typography, and symbols—a visual vocabulary, if you will, that you can use to help tell the story and evoke the emotion that will motivate the consumer. For example, nighttime shows and dramas use a lot of black and rich colors. Daytime shows and comedies use white and bright colors. Children's shows use primary colors. Red is associated with passion, blue with trust. Hospitals and health care companies would avoid red because of the association with blood, but would use blue because it tends to communicate security and wellbeing. Rounded type is playful and would be used for children's products. Chiseled type is classic and strong and might be used for a historical movie such as *Troy*. Sans serif fonts such as Helvetica, are generally considered more contemporary than serif fonts such as Times. Rays of light can evoke a sense of drama, inspiration, power, or metaphysical phenomena. Shadowy figures or objects elicit feelings of mystery or fear.

This project will add these tools and techniques to your growing arsenal:

✔ Alpha channels
✔ Color Picker
✔ Colorize
✔ Curves
✔ Layer styles
✔ Levels
✔ Type tool

Define the job

Your assignment is to create key art for the marketing campaign and package design for a male vocalist. Here is the information you have been given.

ARTIST'S NAME: Ricky Hart

GENRE: Latin Pop

TARGET AUDIENCE: Females 18–34, largely Hispanic but with crossovers to other ethnic groups.

CREATIVE DIRECTION: Create key art that can be used for print ads and CD booklet cover. Build brand by reinforcing Hart's image as a Latin heartthrob. Use rich, passionate imagery that speaks to the Latin culture. Increase audience recognition by using a closeup of artist's face. Broaden audience appeal by using a combination of Spanish and English.

All of this information will inform your choices—what colors to use, the overall look and feel, the emotional response you're going for, what photos of the artist will work best, what fonts to choose, and how to design the type.

It is important when creating key art that you know from the beginning all the ways the final art will be used. The resolution of your key art will be determined by the final usage. You want to avoid sampling up. That means you need to build the original artwork to accommodate the largest size and resolution that will be needed. Normally the ad would be built at 300ppi, but to keep file size down for readers with limited RAM or speed, we will use a resolution of 150ppi.

Set up document and place major elements

MASK RICKY

1. Open the image **Ricky.tif**. Based on the creative direction we have been given, we know we will be using a closeup of Ricky. We won't be using his legs and we don't need all of the white background. This is a case where I'd say it's safe to crop off the excess, thus making the image more manageable. Do a Save As to protect the original in case it's decided later that a full body shot should be used instead of a closeup.

2. To crop the image, choose the Crop tool (**FIGURE 3-1**), marquee the area you wish to preserve, and press Return/Enter or click the checkmark icon in the options bar. Do a Save As, with Photoshop as the format, and name the document *Ricky Masked*.

3. Double-click on the *Background* to convert it into a layer. Give it the name *ricky*. One advantage of stock photography is that it often comes with pre-made alpha channels that you can use to make a selection and separate the object or person from the background. Open the Channels palette and Command/Ctrl-click on the alpha channel provided by the stock photo house (**FIGURE 3-2**).

4. Add a 2-pixel feather, then switch back to the Layers palette and click on the Layer Mask icon to add a layer mask (**FIGURE 3-3**).

We will be using alpha channels in the project. If you are unfamiliar with alpha channels, take a moment to read **Photoshop Essential 3.1: Alpha Channels** at the end of this project.

SET UP THE FINAL DOCUMENT

1. Make a new document 7.25″ x 10.75″ at 150ppi, choosing CMYK for the color mode. Save the document. Name it P3.psd and choose Photoshop from the Format menu.

Crop tool

FIGURE 3-1

FIGURE 3-2

Add Layer Mask

FIGURE 3-3

THE BATTLE: DESIGNERS, COPYWRITERS, MARKETERS AT ODDS

It takes many people to create a successful ad campaign and they don't always see eye to eye. Each person or department brings its own set of priorities and sensibilities to the table. The marketers want to make sure their marketing strategy is adhered to and their message is communicated loud and clear. Copywriters, who labor over every word and nuance, feel their headline and body copy is what will get the reader's attention and sell the product. The designer tends to feel visual impact and cool design is what it's all about. I believe a good ad needs all of these things. People are often drawn to an ad because of the visual impact, but the visual needs to be supported with a strong headline and body copy, together furthering the brand message and advancing the marketing strategy.

Designers may spend hours or days coming up with what they feel to be the perfect design solution, only to have the copywriter or marketing department want to modify the design in ways the designer finds truly objectionable, such as an extremely large and blaring headline that looks completely out of place; or overly strict adherence to traditional rules about layout. As the designer, you need to be able to make an argument in support of your design. Be prepared to give a reasonable explanation for every design decision you make. Marketers often need to be convinced with words and logic. They *want* to be convinced. If your argument is logical and presented with confidence, they may come around to your way of thinking. However, avoid becoming too emotionally invested in your design, and choose carefully what battles you wish to fight. Many times the marketing department will not be convinced by your argument and persisting beyond a point will be futile. You may be able to have your way with the copywriter, but you can almost never win a fight with the marketing department if they are strongly opposed to your point of view. Ultimately your job exists only to help them achieve their objectives and they nearly always have the last word.

Obviously, it is best to develop a good rapport with the writers and marketers. You never know where the spark of genius in an ad campaign will come from. It could come from a great visual, or a great headline or a concept. Any member of the team may be the one to introduce the creative nugget that will develop into a successful campaign. The best work is almost always a collaboration. ■

2. Create a layer group and name it *RICKY HART*.

3. Choose the Move tool and drag the *ricky* layer from Ricky Masked into P3.psd, then close Ricky Masked. Position Ricky in P3.psd so his chin is just above center and his head is cropped on the right side.

4. You need to rotate him to a more upright position. Activate the Free Transform command (Command-T/Ctrl-T), zoom out, and drag open the document window so you can rotate using your mouse or stylus, or enter –10° in the Set Rotation field in the options bar. Press Return/Enter to accept the transformation and then save your document (**FIGURE 3-4**).

Create the background

1. Open **flames.tif**. Rename the *Background* layer *flames*.

2. Working in P3, deselect the RICKY HART group by clicking on the *background* layer. Make a new group in your P3.psd document and name it BACKGROUND.

Tip: If the group RICKY HART or the layer ricky *within that group had been selected when you made the new group, the new group would have become a member of the group RICKY HART. For now, avoid putting groups inside groups.*

3. You will no longer need the layer *Background*, so drag it to the trash at the bottom of the Layers palette. Make sure the group BACKGROUND is selected, then drag the layer *flames* from flames.tif into P3.psd. It will be placed in the BACKGROUND group. Close flames.tif (**FIGURE 3-5**).

4. Position the layer with the lighter part of the flames behind Ricky's head and body. The dark at the top of the image will help the title treatment stand out and the dark running down the left side will visually balance Ricky's body on the right.

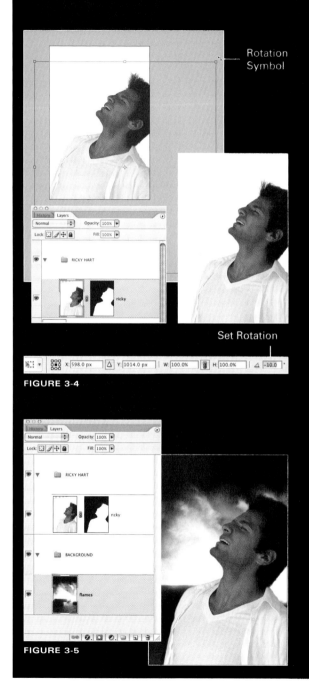

Rotation Symbol

Set Rotation

FIGURE 3-4

FIGURE 3-5

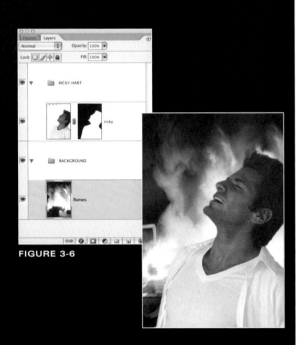

FIGURE 3-6

5. To get the composition I wanted it was necessary to scale the flame layer disproportionately. Since the flames image does not need to be sharply focused or highly realistic, you can get away with distorting it. Press Command-T/Ctrl-T and use the handles to modify the image or enter 77.5% and 130% in the W/H fields in the options bar. Reposition *flames* so the light area is behind Ricky's head. Click the checkmark in the options bar to perform the transformation (**FIGURE 3-6**).

USE A HUE/SATURATION ADJUSTMENT LAYER TO ADD COLOR TO THE BLACK-AND-WHITE *FLAMES* LAYER

One technique used to unify and integrate a composite is to limit the color palette. In this project I have chosen a sepia/gold combination. To me these warm colors say romance, passion, and masculinity, and support Ricky's brand as a Latin heartthrob. In the next steps you will use Hue/Saturation to colorize flames, bringing them into this color palette.

When placed above a color image, a Hue/Saturation adjustment layer can be used to quickly modify colors or to colorize a black-and-white (grayscale) image. The color mode of the image must be changed to either RGB or CMYK to take advantage of this feature. When a grayscale image is converted to RGB either by changing its color mode in the menu or by dragging it into an RGB document, Hue/Saturation has little effect unless you check the *Colorize* box in the lower right corner of the dialog. Colorize makes the image look like a duotone—a mix of two colors—in this case, black and one other color. It isn't necessary to check *Colorize* to add color to a grayscale image that has been converted to CMYK, but checking it can give you a more even duotone look. In the next few steps you will use Hue/Saturation to add color to the flames.

1. Hide the group RICKY HART temporarily so you can concentrate on the background.

2. From the Fill and Adjustment Layers menu at the bottom of the Layers palette, choose Hue/Saturation. The Hue/Saturation dialog opens.

3. Check the **Colorize** box in the lower right. Use the sliders to choose a rich sepia color. The color I chose was composed of Hue 27 at a Saturation of 61. Click OK (**FIGURE 3-7**).

FIGURE 3-7

In the next few steps you will use Levels and Curves adjustment layers to modify the image in various ways. These two types of adjustment layers are critical to nondestructive image manipulation and will be used extensively throughout the remaining projects. If you are new to these features, take a break now and read **Photoshop Essential 3.2: Levels and Curves**.

USE AN ALPHA CHANNEL TO CREATE THE HANDWRITING

1. Open the image **handwriting.tif** (**FIGURE 3-8**). We will use this to add texture to the background. It is a dictionary definition of the word *abandon*. This echoes the title of the CD, *Abandonado*—the Spanish word for having been abandoned. Following the directive to mix Spanish and English, this definition is written in English. The cursive hand adds a human, almost journal-like aspect to the text. I made no attempt to write neatly, the idea being that it seems more human and emotional if it isn't too perfect. I scanned the page as a grayscale halftone.

abandon (ə·ban'dən) v.t. 1) To give up wholly; desert; forsake, as an effort or attempt. 2) To surrender or give over, with to: He abandoned his share to his partner. 3) To yield (oneself) without restraint, as to a feeling or pastime. —n. 1) Utter surrender to one's feelings or natural impulses. 2) Freedom. [<OF abandoner <a bandon under one's own control] — a·ban'don·ment abdicate, abjure, cease, cede, desert, discontinue, forgo, forsake, forswear, leave, quit, recant, relinquish, renounce, repudiate, resign, retreat, surrender, vacate. Denotes the complete and final giving up, letting go, or withdrawal.

FIGURE 3-8

2. With handwriting.tif active, Select All and Copy (Command-C/Ctrl-C). Click P3.psd and open the Channels palette. Click the triangle in the upper right and choose New Channel from the palette menu. In the New Channel dialog, name the channel *handwriting* and **be sure to** check Color Indicates Selected Areas (**FIGURE 3-9**). Click OK. You can close the document handwriting.tif.

FIGURE 3-9

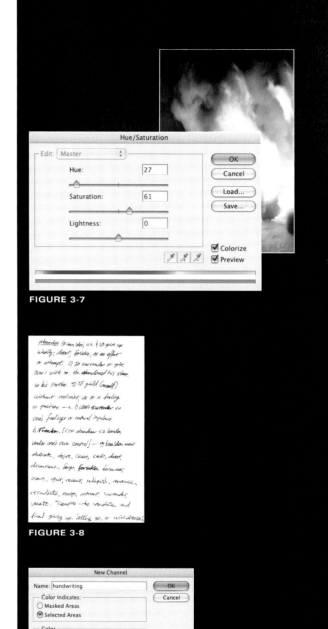

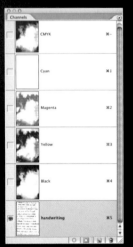

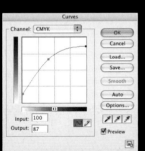

FIGURE 3-10

FIGURE 3-11   **FIGURE 3-12**

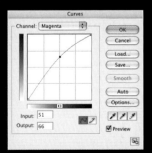

FIGURE 3-13

3. Paste (Command-V/Ctrl-V) the handwriting into the new channel. While the selection is still active, scale the handwriting to 60% and position it so it fills the image area. Unlike layers, channels do not store information in the work area beyond the image window as layers do. Once deselected, all pixels beyond the window will be eliminated, so you want to get it right before committing the transform (**FIGURE 3-10**).

A gotcha: If you didn't discard the original Background layer and you happen to have it selected in the Layers palette, you will not be able to paste into the new alpha channel. Select any other layer and it will work.

4. Command/Ctrl-click the thumbnail of the handwriting in the Channels palette to load it as a selection. This means that the dark areas of the handwriting channel—the writing itself—are now selected. Click the CMYK channel at the top of the Channels palette to activate all channels. Return to the Layers palette (**FIGURE 3-11**).

5. You will use a Curves adjustment layer to make the handwriting appear without making it opaque. The Curves adjustment layer will affect the various values of the layers below differently, creating a "lost and found" look.

   ➤ Choose Curves from the Fill and Adjustment Layers menu. With CMYK selected in the Channel menu at the top of the Curves dialog, add a point to the center of the line and drag up and down to see what happens.

   ➤ To achieve the effect shown, I moved it up and slightly to the left until the input number was about 40 and the output was about 67. The point in the lower-left corner controls the dark values. I moved it up until the output was about 13. If you drag straight up, the input will remain 0. Drag the other point on the far right down keeping the input 100 until output is about 87 (**FIGURE 3-12**). Don't close Curves yet.

➤ Choose Magenta from the Channel menu and, again, add a point and move it so the input is 51 and output is 66 (**FIGURE 3-13**). Now click OK. The adjustment layer uses the active selection to make a layer mask that reveals only the area of the handwriting (**FIGURE 3-14**).

➤ Rename the Curves 1 layer to *Curves 1-writing*. Choose Multiply from the Layer blending modes menu. This will create a translucent effect and cause the areas that overlap dark areas on the layers below to be intensified.

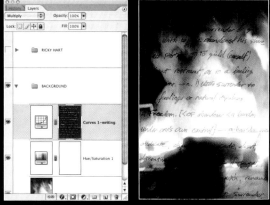
FIGURE 3-14

6. Show the RICKY HART group. For continuity of the background, we want a portion of the handwriting to appear in the light area to the right of Ricky. Duplicate *Curves 1-writing* and move it to the right and down until you are happy with the number of words appearing in that area. Use the Lasso to select around any overlapping words to the left of Ricky and, on the mask, fill the selection with black (**FIGURE 3-15**).

ADD PUNCH BY INCREASING BACKGROUND CONTRAST

To add contrast and richness to the background, add a Levels adjustment layer above *Curves 1-writing copy*. Move the two outside sliders toward the middle to increase contrast. Make the middle tones darker by moving the gray slider to the right. Input readings above the histogram should be approximately 17, 0.78, 233 (**FIGURE 3-16**). Click OK.

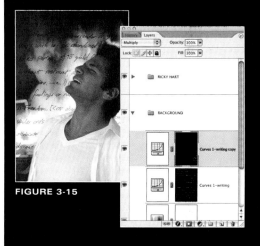
FIGURE 3-15

Integrate the composite

At the moment, Ricky doesn't look integrated with the background. To achieve the look we are after he must actually merge with the background.

Let's start with the shirt. We will use a fill layer to darken the right side, then change the blending mode to allow the background to show through.

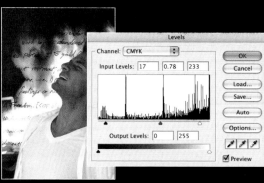
FIGURE 3-16

FIGURE 3-17

FIGURE 3-18

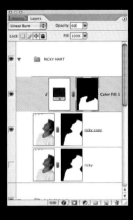

FIGURE 3-19

1. Activate the *ricky* layer. Duplicate *ricky* and hide the original layer temporarily.

2. To darken the shirt, select it by using the Pen tool. **In the options bar be sure to choose *Paths*, not *Shape Layer*, and select *Add to Selection* from the Path areas options buttons**. Create a path along the neckline of his shirt and around his body. You will be taking advantage of the Layer Clipping Mask feature, so the path only needs to be accurate along the neckline. Zoom in close while working on the neckline then zoom out to do the body (**FIGURE 3-17**).

3. When you have closed the path, load it as a selection and add a 2-pixel feather. Press Option/Alt and choose Solid Color from the fill and adjustment layer menu. In the New Layer dialog check **Use Previous Layer to Create Clipping Mask** and click OK. When the Color Picker appears, choose a dark color from within the image and click OK. You now have a flat dark brown area covering the shirt (**FIGURE 3-18**).

4. You may need to clean up the mask along the neckline with a small brush. Try a soft airbrush, 9 pixels in diameter, with the flow set at 20%. Using white, work your way around the neckline going back and forth, gradually revealing and blending the edge of the *Color Fill 1* layer into the shadow along the neckline. There should be no white edges showing. The hint of a dark line along the neckline will be unavoidable. Reduce the Layer opacity to 60% and change the blend mode to Linear Burn (**FIGURE 3-19**). The shirt is now tinted brown.

5. Mask the left side of the *Color Fill 1* layer by choosing the Gradient tool. Select Foreground to Transparent from the Gradient Editor, Radial Gradient, and Transparency from the options bar. Be sure your foreground color is black. Begin just outside the shoulder on the left and drag down toward the center of his chest. This will cause the solid color layer to disappear in that area and create a sense of light (**FIGURE 3-20**).

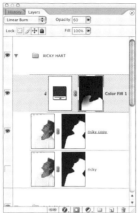

FIGURE 3-20

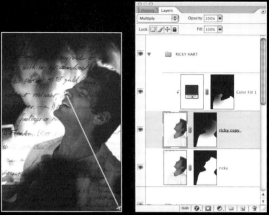

FIGURE 3-21

6. Show the original *ricky* layer. Change the blending modes of *ricky* and *ricky copy* to **Multiply**. This adds richness and intensifies the darks. But it also blends him with the layers below and makes his face too dark. No worries, we'll take of this. Using the Radial Gradient again and working on the layer mask of *ricky copy*, start to the left of his nose and drag down to the lower right corner of the image window. This will lighten his face (**FIGURE 3-21**).

7. The blending modes have helped integrate Ricky with the background, but also allowed the handwriting to show through his face. We don't want this. Working on the layer masks for *curves 1-writing* and *curves 1-writing copy,* use a brush and black to conceal the handwriting that is in or near the face. Reduce the amount of writing showing through the body. Leave some of it to help integrate him with the background (**FIGURE 3-22**). Save your document.

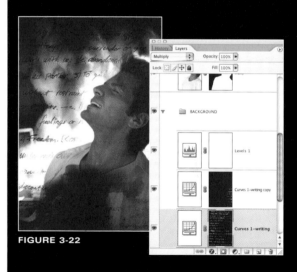

FIGURE 3-22

Tip: When using a brush to fine-tune your masks, you may find it easier if Brush Dynamics is disabled. Use F5 to access the Brushes palette and make sure Brush Dynamics is unchecked. Be careful when working on an adjustment layer mask. You can't simply paint with white to reveal the type again. You will need to reload the selection first or use History to revert to a previous state.

FIGURE 3-23

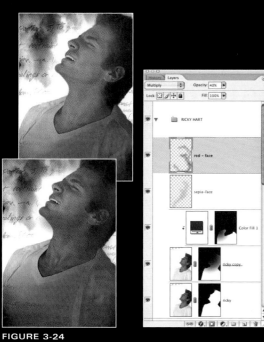

FIGURE 3-24

USE PAINT LAYERS TO CONTROL BACKGROUND SHOW-THROUGH

Refer to **FIGURE 3-23** as you do the next three steps. At the moment Ricky's body looks too transparent. The dark blotchy areas in his shirt and forehead are distracting and cause him to appear too de-constructed, not solid. We need to correct this.

1. Above *flames* add a new layer named *white under body*. With Airbrush selected and a flow of about 10%, paint with white and slowly reduce the dark areas in his shirt and on his face. Don't completely eliminate them. They will help integrate the overall composite and add a gritty quality.

2. Add another layer named *sepia behind back* and choose a sepia color that matches the mid-value areas of the flames. Paint in the area behind Ricky's back to introduce some of the sepia color of the flames into this area and tie things together.

3. The angled object on the far left is also distracting. Add another layer and use dark brown to eliminate it.

USE COLOR TO UNIFY THE COMPOSITE

Next you will use paint layers to help integrate Ricky with the background and add dimension to his face. Areas that would normally be highlighted should not be covered with paint. This is a very subjective move and at first your painting may appear clumsy and heavy-handed. With the use of layer masks to clean up your brushwork, the lowering of layer opacity, and changing of blend-ing modes, the painting will end up much more subtle. To help you see what to do, **FIGURE 3-24** illustrates these layers at 100% opacity and on Normal blending modes.

1. Add two layers above *color fill 1*. Change the blending mode of each layer to Multiply. On the lower of the two, with an air-brush set at 70% flow, use a sepia color (C=5, M=47, Y=89, K=5) and loosely paint over Ricky's forehead, cheeks, neck, and shirt, overlapping the background in places.

2. Choose red (C=0, M=89, Y=99, K=0) and, on the next layer, add color randomly to the face and shirt, again overlapping some of the background. In both steps avoid the front of his face.

3. Use layer masks to conceal paint on his cheekbones, brow, and nose. Reduce layer opacity to make the effect more subtle. I reduced the opacity of the red layer to 40% and the sepia layer to 75%.

INCREASE INTENSITY AND ADD DIMENSION

1. Increase the overall intensity still more by adding another Curves adjustment layer above the red paint layer. Increase the contrast in the CMYK composite channel pane by adding a control point either side of center. Move the right point up and the left one down. This move should be pretty subtle to avoid too strong a color shift. Then choose the yellow channel and modify the yellow in a similar manner. Click OK. Adjust the opacity of the Curves adjustment layer to your liking (**FIGURE 3-25**). I lowered it to 70%.

2. To draw attention to Ricky's face and give it more dimension, we will add highlights to his cheekbones and brow. A couple of very bright spots judiciously placed will create the sense of spotlights and a slight perspiration, which will add to the intensity of his performance and emotion. Add another Curves adjustment layer. Move the middle of the curve down to lighten the image and click OK (**FIGURE 3-26**).

3. At first this adjustment lightens the entire composite. To control where the effect of the adjustment layer is seen, fill the Curves mask with black. Then, use a soft brush and white paint to reveal the effect of the adjustment layer only on his cheekbones, nose, chin, and brow (**FIGURE 3-27**).

4. On a new layer use a small brush (9-pixel diameter) and white paint to add three bright highlights. The largest one should be on his cheekbone, another smaller one on his brow, and one on his nose. Add a mask and zoom in close. Use an airbrush about

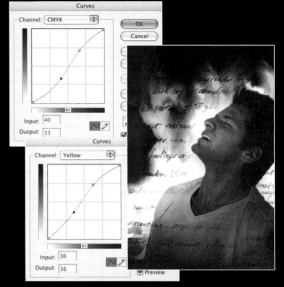

FIGURE 3-25

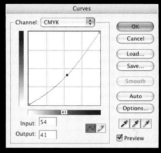

FIGURE 3-26

FIGURE 3-27

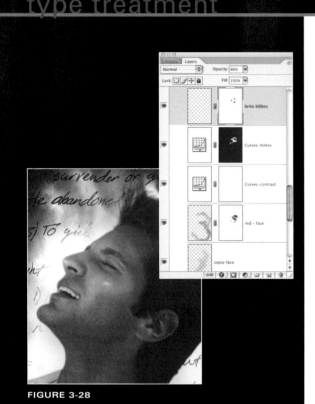

FIGURE 3-28

20 pixels in diameter with flow set at 40% and black to shape and soften the edges of these highlights. Reduce the opacity to 87% (**FIGURE 3-28**). Done properly these small bright highlights can be the *pièce de résistance*, whether on someone's face or the fender of a car. But overdone or left unrefined, they can look very amateurish. If in doubt, use fewer or none at all.

Type treatment

If you are new to the Type tool or Layer styles, take time now to do **Mini-Tutorial 3: Type and Styles** at the end of the project.

In this part of the project we will use the Type tool and Layer styles to add the artist's name, the name of the CD, and a line of information about when the CD will available—the *street date*. Of course, the choices of fonts and the design of the typography are myriad. If this were a real job you would most likely go through many variations before you settled on something you liked. You'd present the best of these to your design director and marketing V.P. After further selection and refinement, one or two of them would be presented along with totally different concepts to the person with final approval authority. That might be an executive V.P., or even the president. Then it would be presented to the artist and his management people for approval.

As you approach the design of the typography you need to keep a few things in mind. From now on, don't think of type as merely a means of dispensing information. Think of it also as a design element. Come up with ways to integrate the type into the composite, but don't lose legibility in the process. Look for ways to use contrast in scale and style to add interest. Always keep in mind the things we talked about at the beginning of this project: What are you trying to say, and to whom are you saying it? How will your design support and enhance the branding of the product—Ricky Hart? What typestyle will elicit the emotion you want and help tell the story?

I chose the font Trajan Pro for *HART*. A classic font, it speaks to Ricky's Latin heritage and is stylish and elegant without being feminine. Its formal structure contrasts with the handwritten script in the background. Trajan Pro has only uppercase letters, initial capitals being distinguished from the other letters by size. To add more contrast the title of the CD, *Abandonado*, is set in a simple Helvetica. The clean lines of this sans serif font contrast without conflicting with the serif font, Trajan Pro.

There is a saying—"You can get as much attention with a whisper as with a shout in the right situation." By its placement in a fairly empty area, in a contrasting color, and in a relatively small point size, "Abandonado" gets attention and doesn't compete with "Hart." A glow ties it in with the whole illuminated, burning motif.

Feel free to experiment with fonts of your own choosing. Since the type tool is vector-based you can change the font at any time without compromising the quality.

FIGURE 3-29

CREATE *HART*

1. Select the RICKY HART group and create a new group above it named TYPE. From the type tools select the Horizontal Type tool. Choose a font you like. The appropriate point size will vary depending on the font. I used Trajan Pro at 189 points. For now, choose a light color that is easy to see; we will modify the color later. Click near the top of the image and type *Hart*. Use the Move tool to drag it into place. If you are using a font other than Trajan Pro, you can get the effect of the larger initial cap by selecting the H and increasing the point size to about 230 (**FIGURE 3-29**).

2. Open the Character palette by clicking the *Toggle the Character and Paragraph palettes* button in the options bar. Adjust the kerning—place the cursor between two letters and reduce the amount of space by choosing one of the presets from the kerning menu or by typing an amount in the kerning field. The

FIGURE 3-30

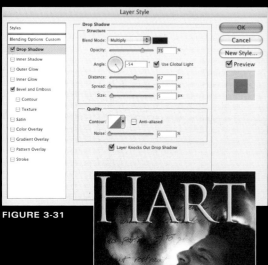

FIGURE 3-31

amount of kerning necessary will vary among fonts. It is usually necessary to adjust the kerning on either side of A's and T's. It is especially important to adjust kerning on large type such as this. After kerning, center the type horizontally in the image window (**FIGURE 3-30**).

3. From the Styles menu, choose Bevel and Emboss. From Style choose Inner Bevel, from Technique choose Smooth. Set the depth to 191, direction Up, size 8, soften 1. In the Shading pane set the Angle to about –54, the Attitude to 42, and Global Light on. Increase the opacity for both Highlight and Shadow to 100% (**FIGURE 3-31**). Click OK.

4. Now change the color of the type. Highlight the type by dragging across it or double-clicking the T icon in the Layers palette. Click the color swatch in either the options bar or the Character palette. When the Color Picker appears, move your cursor over the image and choose a dark brown from the background. Click OK. Click the checkmark in the options bar. Lower the Layer opacity to 65% (**FIGURE 3-32**).

5. To light up the top part of the type and separate it from the background, Option/Alt-click the New Layer button at the bottom of the Layers palette. In the dialog name the layer *type highlight* and check **Use Previous Layer to Create Clipping Mask,** then click OK. Select a large, soft brush (200 pixels in diameter). Choose Airbrush in the options bar, reduce the Flow to 40% and choose one of the gold colors from within the image. Paint with strokes going from top to bottom at about a 45-degree angle across the type. Add more paint at the top to make it stand out. You may want to try this a couple of times on different layers until you get an effect you like. When you have a layer you like, drag the unwanted layers to the trash. Duplicate the layer to increase the effect (**FIGURE 3-33**).

FIGURE 3-32

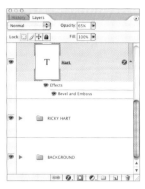

FIGURE 3-33

FIGURE 3-34

6. Add a layer mask to the type layer, *hart*, and mask the part of the R and T that overlap Ricky's hair. This will make it look as if Ricky is in front of the type (**FIGURE 3-34**).

7. The bright spot behind his head at the bottom of the T is distracting and needs to be toned down. In the BACKGROUND group add a new layer above *sepia behind back* and name it *darken behind head*. Choose one of the medium-value colors near the T and paint out the white area (**FIGURE 3-35**).

CREATE *ABANDONADO*

1. Click the TYPE group to make it active and select the Horizontal Type tool. Choose a medium weight sans serif font, make the size about 15.5 points and the color white. Type the word *ABANDONADO*, all uppercase, in the lower-third area of the composition. Open the tracking to 700. Click the checkmark in the options bar.

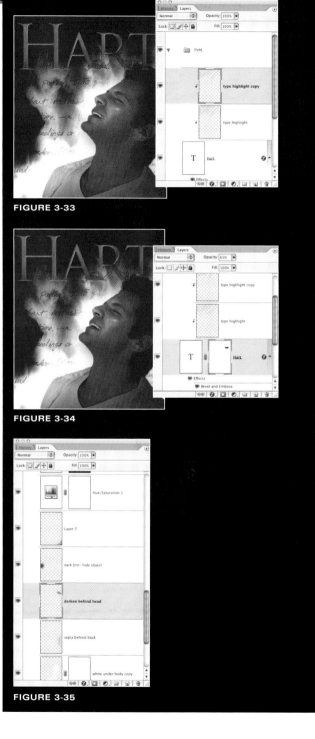

FIGURE 3-35

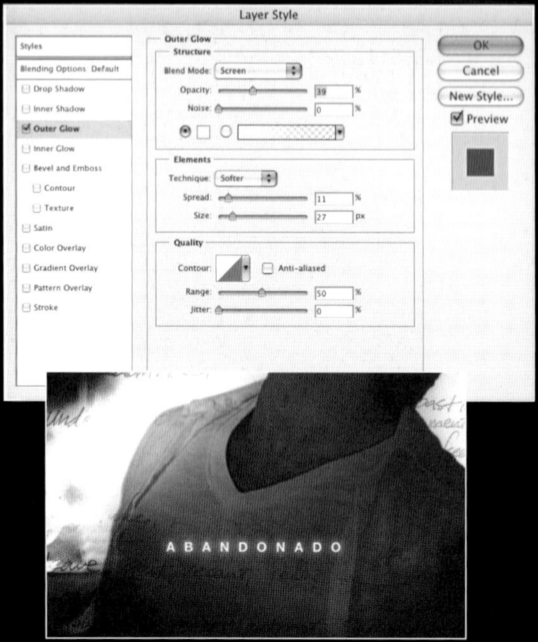

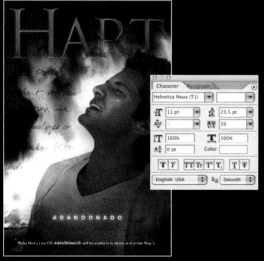

FIGURE 3-36

FIGURE 3-37

2. From the layer styles menu at the bottom of the Layers palette choose Outer Glow. Set the opacity to 39, the spread to 11, and size to 27. Leave the other settings at their defaults and click OK (**FIGURE 3-36**).

ADD THE MARKETING INFORMATION

Unfortunately, there is always a lot of marketing information, legal lines, and logos that need to be included on print ads and posters. Designers always hate this stuff because it messes up the design. Some of it imparts important information for the consumer; some of it merely satisfies the lawyers. For our ad we will just include a single line about when the CD will be released.

With the Type tool still selected, change the point size to 11; Helvetica medium or any similar simple font will do. Use white and type "Ricky Hart's new CD, *ABANDONADO*, will be available in stores and online May 5." Move this line to the bottom of the composition and center it (**FIGURE 3-37**).

USING THE KEY ART IN OTHER CONFIGURATIONS

This key art will be used throughout the print campaign and on the packaging. Making the key art work in various configurations can be very challenging. The goal is to maintain as much as possible the original look and feel.

This key art will require very little modification for full-page ads, because the aspect ratio is very close to that of most magazines. A little resizing and minor shifting of elements is all that will be needed. Half-page ads, either vertical or horizontal, will be more challenging. **FIGURE 3-38** shows one possible solution.

FIGURE 3-39 is one possible layout for the CD booklet cover. Ricky's head and name have maintained the same relationship. But, the relative size of ABANDONADO has been changed. ABANDONADO has been darkened to read in the white area and the tracking has been decreased to make it more legible at the smaller point size and to prevent it from pushing into Ricky's neck. The background was reduced to keep the same flame-like feel.

FIGURE 3-38

FIGURE 3-39

The Channels palette looks much like the Layers palette, but channels and layers are very different things. Each of the colors in your document exists on a separate plane or band. These planes are called channels. There are three channels for RGB, four for CMYK, and only one channel for a grayscale image. In an RGB document these relate to the three passes of a scanner; in CMYK to the plates used on a press (**PE 3.1A**). Each channel is actually a grayscale representation of the distribution of a color throughout the image, ranging in values from 0 to 255. When combined, Photoshop uses this information to generate the millions of colors it can create. At the top of the Channels palette is the composite channel, which is not really a channel at all, but indicates that all the channels are active. You can view the channels separately or in any combination.

The Channels palette will display information only for layers that are currently visible. If a layer is currently hidden, the information on that layer will not appear.

In addition to the color channels there are two other types: spot channels and alpha channels. Normally, when an image is printed, the different colors are created by combining varying amounts of cyan, magenta, yellow, and black ink (CMYK). These are called *process colors*. Occasionally, you will find it useful to print part of your image with an ink that is a specific color (for example, if the color is part of your company's branding). Such a color is called a *spot color*. Creating and using spot channels is quite tricky and beyond the scope of this project. Alpha channels are something you should know about and take advantage of.

Alpha channels store information that is used for masking and selections. Alpha channels do not affect the color of the image in any way and will not print when the document is sent to output. The information for all layer masks and saved selections is stored in alpha channels. However, you will only see the alpha channel for a layer mask listed on the Channels palette if that layer is currently active. When you highlight a different layer, that alpha channel will no longer be visible. Alpha channels can be created in several ways—by saving a selection, duplicating an existing color channel, or by creating a New Channel from the Channels palette menu.

Alpha channels are so valuable and such fun when it comes to selections because of their ability to make intricate selections with a single click. You have already learned that you can load a layer as a

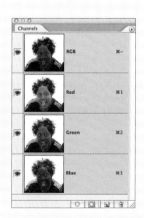

PE 3.1A

PE 3.1B

PE 3.1C

PE 3.1D

PE 3.1E

selection by Command/Ctrl-clicking on the layer in the Layers palette. The selection is determined by the visible pixels on that layer. If the layer contains a full-frame image, you get a selection framing the image (**PE 3.1B**).

An alpha channel or any of the color channels can be loaded as a selection in the same way, but with a very different result. If you Command/Ctrl-click on an alpha channel you get a selection based on the grayscale values of the channel. **PE 3.1C** illustrates a selection I made by Command/Ctrl-clicking on the red channel of this RGB image. The areas of darker value (referred to as *color* in the New Channel dialog) become either the masked area or the selected area depending on the last choice made in the New Channel dialog (**PE 3.1D**).

This means areas of great detail can be quickly selected, providing there is enough contrast between the areas you wish to select and their surroundings. This is a good way to select someone's hair, for example, if they have been photographed against a solid light background. In this example I duplicated the cyan channel, which automatically created an alpha channel. I increased the contrast of the new alpha channel using Levels. This created the equivalent of a stencil. I then loaded the alpha as a selection and added a layer mask (**PE 3.1E**). You will use an alpha channel in this project to quickly select Ricky's body and mask out the background. You will use another one to create a complex selection of handwritten text and use that selection in combination with an adjustment layer for an interesting textural effect. In Project 5 you will use an alpha channel to select a very intricate chain-link fence and use the selection to create an interesting posterized effect.

The ability to modify value, contrast, and color is at the core of digital imaging. Whether creating dramatic effects or doing simple color corrections, the weapons of choice are the Levels or Curves adjustments. Both can be applied via adjustment layers. That means they are totally nondestructive and always editable. To develop proficiency, particularly with Curves, may take a while; but even at a basic level they greatly enhance your ability to manipulate images. This overview will give you what you need to get you started. You can do pretty much the same things with either Levels or Curves.

The Curves dialog does offer greater control, but at the cost of greater complexity. The accompanying figures compare how the same result was achieved using each type of adjustment. Refer to them as you read the text.

The Levels dialog is divided into two parts: Input and Output. The Input area includes a *histogram* which represents the distribution of lights and darks throughout the image (**PE 3.2A**). The horizontal axis of the histogram has 256 values because most images use 8-bit color, technically that means that the maximum number of levels of intensity in each channel is a number eight binary digits long. The value of this number is 2 raised to the power of 8, which equals 256. Therefore, each channel in the image has 256 discrete levels of intensity. This is at the core of digital imaging, and is the result of various decisions made in the design of modern computer operating systems and applications. The Channel menu at the top of the dialog tells which channel you are modifying. When the composite channel is selected, you are modifying contrast and brightness by changing the distribution of values (darks and lights) throughout the image. The left end of the histogram represents the darkest values in the image and the right end the lightest. By moving the left (black) Input slider to the right you force middle-values areas toward black; by moving the right (white) slider to the left you force shades toward white, thereby increasing the contrast. The middle (gray) slider controls the middle values; move it to the left and you lighten the image, to the right and you darken the image. Be careful, though—very large moves can result in significant color shifts (**PE 3.2B**).

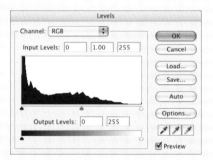

PE 3.2A

Channel menu   Histogram

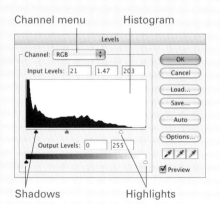

PE 3.2B   Shadows   Highlights

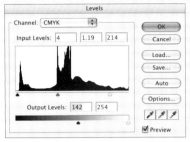

PE 3.2C

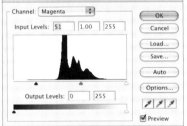
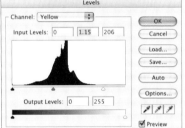

PE 3.2D

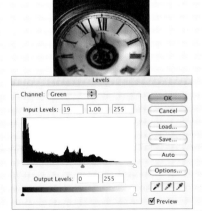
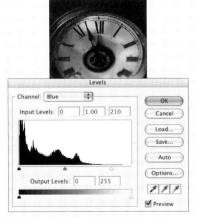

PE 3.2E

At the bottom of the Levels dialog is the Output area, containing a bar that enables control of the overall brightness. Move the black slider to the right and all of the values in the image become darker, move the white slider to the left and the opposite happens (**PE 3.2C**).

As useful and important as the Levels dialog is for controlling contrast and brightness, the real magic happens when you use it on individual channels. You can change the color of the image by modifying the distribution of values for a particular channel. This is one way color corrections are done. For example, if you wish to make an image less yellow and more magenta and you are working in CMYK mode, you would choose the magenta channel and move the black slider to the right to increase the dark values in that channel, then go to the yellow channel and move the white slider to the left to increase the light values in that channel and reduce the amount of yellow in the image (**PE 3.2D**). Think of red, green, and blue as the opposites of cyan, magenta, and yellow on the color wheel. To get the same results in RGB mode, you would go to the green channel and move the black slider to right to increase the amount of magenta. To modify the yellow, go to the blue channel and move the white slider to the left. This takes a little getting used to. Just remember RGB = CMY (**PE 3.2E**).

As mentioned earlier, the Curves dialog is a pretty complicated piece of software. But you don't need to know everything about it to start using it and have some fun. When you first open the Curves dialog you see a straight line—the curve—running diagonally across a grid. You modify the values in the image by clicking the curve to add a point and

continues...

then dragging the point to a new location. The gradated bar across the bottom tells you which value you are changing and the bar on the left tells what you have changed it to (**PE 3.2F**). If you are working in CMYK, the default status of the dialog is that the right side of the grid represents the darker values and the left side the lighter values. If you are working in RGB it is the reverse. To increase the contrast as we did with Levels, add a point to the upper right side and move it up and slightly right (if working in CMYK, reverse this procedure). That will increase

the range of dark values in the image. Add another to the left side and move it down and to the left to increase the range of light values (**PE 3.2G**).

To increase the amount of magenta, select the magenta channel. Add a point in the middle of the curve and move it up. To decrease the amount of yellow, go to the yellow channel, add a point in the middle and move it down (**PE 3.2H**). For RGB images, remember RGB = CMY and you will know which channel you need to choose to modify a specific color.

As you progress through the remaining projects you will learn more about the power of Levels and Curves and how to use them to enhance your composites.

Channel menu

Curve

Point tool

PE 3.2F

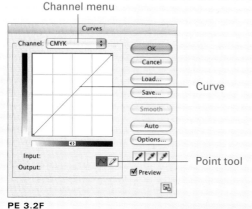

PE 3.2G

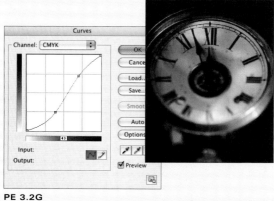

PE 3.2H

mini-tutorial 3

Type tool and Layer styles

Begin thinking of type not merely as a way to delineate words and dispense information, but as a graphic design element in and of itself. From now on, whenever you look at type, think about the way the letters are formed and how the type has been configured on the page. What is the personality of the particular type? How does the type help tell the story? Why did the designer pick that font and why was it handled in that way? Has the type been manipulated in any way to enhance the design or evoke a feeling? Was legibility sacrificed for the sake of design, or vice versa? Look for ways to integrate the type with the ad. Avoid having type that looks like an afterthought, something that was stuck on the image at the last minute. From the outset you should plan the ad to accommodate the type in an interesting and effective way.

We'll begin this tutorial with the image of a battleship and add the word *BATTLE*. By way of font selection and Photoshop techniques, and the illusion of looking through binoculars, we will create a "title" that illustrates what is happening and evokes an immediate emotional response.

Photoshop's Type tool is powerful and versatile. It produces vector-based type, which means it is resolution independent—it can be scaled without losing quality and it can be edited at any time. Also, since it is vector, if the document is printed on a PostScript printer, the edges will come out crisp and clean. At one time, images for an ad were created in Photoshop then flattened and brought into a publishing program such as QuarkXpress or a drawing program such as Illustrator to do the type. Today, thanks to the vector-based Type tool, many designers create their entire ad in Photoshop. The one caveat is that for the vector technology to work you must output to a PostScript printer or first output to PDF; then you can print to a non-PostScript printer. One really cool thing about creating type in Photoshop is that you can apply layer styles to the type. Each layer style is a collection of special effects, such as bevel and emboss, drop shadows, and many more. These allow you to greatly enhance the ad and increase production value.

The Type tool has four variations: two vector-based tools and two that are for making selections only. To keep your edit options open and maintain resolution independence, you must select one of the vector tools. The Horizontal Type tool is by far the most useful. This tool's options bar provides you with a variety of information and choices, but the real editing power is in the Character and Paragraph palettes. These contain everything that is in the options bar and much more. To open these palettes click the *Toggle the Character and Paragraph palettes* button in the options bar.

Let's look at the Character palette.

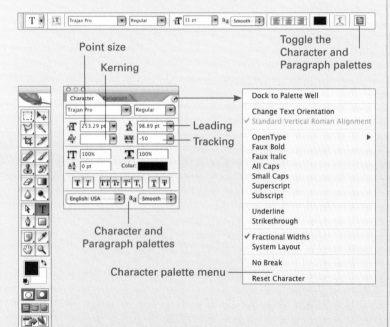

Point size

Kerning

Toggle the
Character and
Paragraph palettes

Leading

Tracking

Character and
Paragraph palettes

Character palette menu

Dock to Palette Well

Change Text Orientation
✓ Standard Vertical Roman Alignment

OpenType ▶
Faux Bold
Faux Italic
All Caps
Small Caps
Superscript
Subscript

Underline
Strikethrough

✓ Fractional Widths
System Layout

No Break

Reset Character

SET THE TYPE

1. Open the image **Ship.tif**. Double-click the *Background* and rename it *ship*.

2. Choose the Horizontal Type tool. Open the Character palette and choose a heavy-weight font, such as Machine or Impact, about 185 points (the size can easily be changed later). Leading (the space between lines of type) doesn't matter since there will be only one word. Tracking should be 0 (zero). Click on the color swatch, move your cursor over the image and choose a dark blue-gray from the ship. Choosing a color from within the image right away begins to integrate the type with background. Click in the image window and type *BATTLE*. A new Type layer has just been added to the Layers palette. Click the checkmark button in the options bar to deselect the type.

3. The characters of our alphabet have a wide variety of shapes. This causes the spacing between some letters to look too narrow or too wide compared to the spacing between other

letters in the word. It is often necessary, especially when working with large point sizes, to modify the spacing manually to compensate for this variation. The spacing between two letters is called *kerning*. This is often confused with *tracking*, which is the space between multiple letters. Tracking would apply to an entire word or line; it's more global while kerning is more local. Hide *ship* for a moment. The space (kerning) between B and A is a little "open" or wide compared to the other letters. To close it, place your cursor between the B and the A and reduce the amount of kerning by choosing –10 from the kerning menu in the Character palette. Place your cursor between the A and T and reduce the kerning by –10. Place the cursor between the two T's and increase the kerning by 10. When you've finished improving the appearance of the type, click the check button in the options bar to confirm your changes.

Tip: In addition to modifying both kerning and tracking by choosing from the presets, or manually entering amounts in the fields, you can drag on the pictorial label (the letters with the small arrows) next to the field for each item to increase or decrease the specified amount.

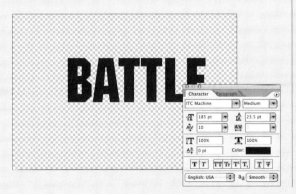

ADD DIMENSION WITH LAYER STYLES

Layer styles are a great way to add instant depth and dimension to your type.

Make the ship layer visible again, but keep the BATTLE layer selected.

1. Open the layer style dialog (in the Layers palette double-click in the area next to the layer name or click the *f* button at the bottom of the Layers palette) and choose an effect from the menu. Click the name of an effect to access the options for that effect. Click Bevel and Emboss.

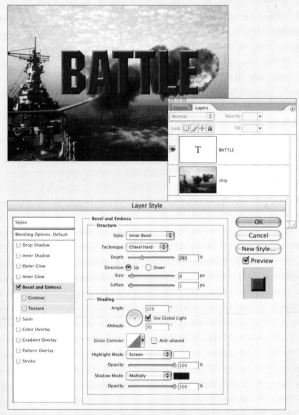

2. From the Style menu choose Inner Bevel. From Technique choose Chisel Hard. This will give the letters a more machine-like look, and help relate the type to the warship. When adding a 3D style, pay attention to the light source in the photograph. Maintaining a consistent light source will help hold the illustration together and integrate the type with the background. So, in this case, the Direction should be Up. I used Size 8, soften 1 for this figure. Play around with Depth, Size, and Soften until you get something you like.

3. In the Shading pane, adjust the angle of the light, if necessary, by clicking on the cross-hairs in the little circle and rotating them to the appropriate position. *Use Global Light* will keep the light source consistent if you apply additional styles. Highlight mode can stay on Screen. Click the color swatch next to the Highlight mode and choose a light color from within the photograph. Increase the opacity to 100%. Shadow Mode can stay on Multiply and, again, click the swatch and choose a dark color from within the image. Increase the opacity to 100%.

4. Click Outer Glow in the Styles on the left. In the Structure pane, click the color swatch and choose an orange from the fireball in the photo. Change the Blend Mode to Linear Burn and the Opacity to 56%. In the Elements pane, leave the Technique on Softer and change the Spread to 9 and Size to 40. Click OK to close the Layer Style dialog.

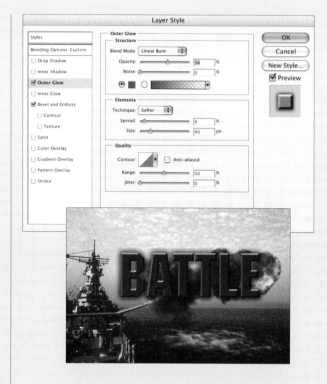

5. At the top of the Layers palette just below Opacity is Fill. Lowering fill can reduce the opacity of the object on a layer (in this case the type) without lowering the opacity of the styles. Lower fill to 30%.

6. To add a distressed, war-torn look, add a layer mask and select the Brush tool. From the Brushes Presets, choose Stipple 29 (choose view as Large or Small List from the Presets menu to help you find it). Increase the diameter to 60 and, working on the layer mask using black, click at various places on the letters.

Tip: Click the triangle next to the f in the Layers palette to show the effects currently applied to a layer. Click the eye next to Style *to hide or show individual effects.*

CREATE THE BINOCULAR EFFECT
To help tell the story and focus attention, now create the effect of looking through binoculars.

1. Add a new layer named *binoculars* and fill it with black. Use the Elliptical marquee, press Option/Alt, start to drag and then press Shift to make a circular selection on the left side of the composition. Pressing Option/Alt while creating a selection will make the first place you click the center of your selection; Shift will constrain the selection to a perfect circle. Option/Alt-Click the Add a Layer Mask button at the bottom of the Layers palette.

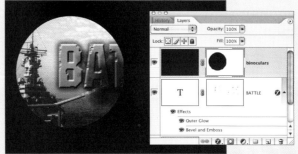

2. Command/Ctrl-click the mask thumbnail in the Layers palette to load the mask as a selection. Inverse the selection (Selection > Inverse). With the Marquee tool selected, drag the selection to the right side of the composition. Fill the selection with black. Deselect and add an 18.5-pixel Gaussian blur. Use Transform to enlarge the layer if necessary to get the desired effect.

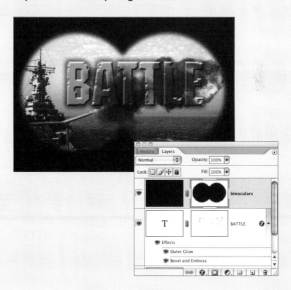

INTENSIFY THE EXPLOSION

Add intensity and drama with a red gradient layer.

Above *ship*, make a new layer named *red sky*.
Choose the Gradient tool, select Linear Gradient
from Gradient styles, and Foreground to Transparent from the presets in the Gradient Editor. With
a red-orange as the foreground color start at the
upper right edge of the right binocular circle and
drag toward lower center of the image. Release the
mouse button about an inch from the lower edge of
the document window. Change the blending mode
to Hard Light. You've created a title graphic with
intensity, drama, and focus that says to the viewer,
"there's excitement here."

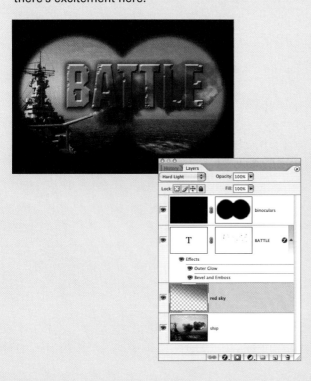

outdoor ad
CAMPAIGN OUTDOOR AD CAMPAIGN OUTDOOR AD CAMPAIGN OUTDOOR

campaign

OUTDOOR AD CAMPAIGN

OUTDOOR ADVERTISING IS AN IMPORTANT COMPONENT of any national marketing campaign for a television program or motion picture. Typical outdoor campaigns include multiple venues and formats. Familiarize yourself with the media buy and specifications before you begin. Then, create your key art for the largest size. Once it's approved, you will use that artwork to create all of the other configurations.

4

project description

Create a 14′ x 48′ billboard, called a Bulletin, for an outdoor advertising campaign. This will be the key art for an outdoor campaign launching a new television sitcom, *Alpha Male*. The campaign will be concentrated in three major markets—New York, Chicago, and Los Angeles. The media buy will include billboards, bus sides, transit shelters, and shopping mall kiosks. Your design must be equally effective whether viewed from 50 feet or 3 feet.

design direction

Illustrate in a playful way a relationship in which the man thinks he is in charge but is actually being affectionately manipulated by his spouse. Establish audience recognition of the stars and create a logo that will brand the show.

assets

"Selects"—photos of the show's stars that have been approved for use in advertising and promotions—have been provided and include a head shot of the male lead and three of the female lead. A body double was photographed in a playful kick pose. You have been instructed to incorporate this image into the logo in some way if possible. The head of the show's female star will have to be composited onto the double's body.

With those assets you will use these tools and techniques:

- ✔ Clone Stamp tool
- ✔ Color Correction
- ✔ Healing Brush
  - ✔ Spot Healing Brush
    - ✔ Mix and match body parts
      - ✔ Retouching using a paint layer with a grain overlay
      - ✔ Shape Layers
      - ✔ Shape tools
      - ✔ Vector masks

OUTDOOR ADVERTISING—A MEDIUM IN ITS OWN RIGHT

Outdoor advertising is unlike any other advertising medium. It can be very effective, delivering high viewer memory retention and product recognition. Or it can be totally ineffective and a huge waste of money.

Here are some pointers that will make your outdoor advertising more effective.

➤ **Keep it simple.** For the highest degree of memory retention, the idea should be clear and simple. Make use of surprise, humor, or drama. The ad will have greater memory retention if it entertains and intrigues.

➤ **Make the type easy to read.** Type must be legible at a glance from a distance. Very often you have only a few seconds to get your message across. The type needs to be larger than you might expect or find attractive. Choose fonts that are easy to read. The fonts should be bold, but not too bold—from a distance letters set in very heavy type become indistinguishable from one another. The fonts should not be overly designed, overly compressed, or overly ornamental. If a serif font is used, it should be one that doesn't have extreme changes between the thick and thin portions of the letters. Upper- and lowercase words are considered easier to read. All-uppercase words can have a strong impact, but should be used for only a few words or a very short sentence.

➤ **Choose colors wisely.** Use colors that are appropriate for the genre and that support the emotional thrust of the campaign. For easy viewability, the colors should be strong in contrast—both value and hue. Complementary colors (opposites on the color wheel) always work well together, but make sure they are of significantly different values so they are easily differentiated well from a distance.

➤ **Stand out from the crowd.** There are certain things you can do to embellish and draw attention to your ad, such as 3D elements, moving parts, and extending the image beyond the borders. Of these, the most common is the use of extensions. Breaking the frame of a billboard with the top of a head, other body part, or object immediately creates a more dynamic ad. Of course, this will add considerably to the production costs.

➤ **Frequency.** Although the viewer may be see your ad for only a few seconds, repeated exposure will insure that your message is absorbed and retained. To accomplish this most campaigns will include multiple venues and formats within a single market. A person may be exposed to a couple of billboards, a transit shelter, and a mall kiosk all in one day. To avoid viewer fatigue and memory decline, multiple variations on the design or concept may be used. Be sure the variations all have the same look and feel. You want the viewer to immediately make the connection between the ads.

FIGURE 4-1

FIGURE 4-2

FIGURE 4-3

Create a billboard in five stages

1. Mask out the backgrounds on each of the main images you will use.

2. Create the final document and place these images to get a feel for the overall layout.

3. Create the title logo and network logo using the Type and Shape tools. Also, with the Type tool, set the headline and tune-in information.

4. Once all the major elements are in place, use Photoshop's retouching tools to correct flaws and enhance the appearances of the show's stars.

5. In the final step, put the female star's head on the body of the kicking woman and make color corrections so the body matches the head.

MASK THE TALENT

1. Open the image **Leo.tif**. Double-click on *background* and rename it *leo*.

2. Make a new group named *LEO* and move the layer leo into the group LEO (**FIGURE 4-1**). If you skipped Project 2 and are un-comfortable working with the Pen tool, stop now and do **Mini-Tutorial 2: Creating paths with the Pen tool** in Project 2. Use the Pen tool to make a path around Leo. Around the hair be sure to get some of the spiky bits, but don't go nuts. The top of Leo's head is going to extend beyond the top of the billboard. That portion will be supported by a separate attachment that will be cut out in the shape of the hair, so the silhouette of the hair needs to be relatively simple. When you are satisfied with the path, make it into a selection, add a 2-pixel feather, then add a layer mask (**FIGURE 4-2**). Save the image as Leo.psd.

3. Repeat these steps on the image **Kristin1.tif**. Don't forget to mask out the space between her hand and her cheek. Eliminate the small portion of dress showing on her back (**FIGURE 4-3**).

MECHANICAL SPECIFICATIONS FOR OUTDOOR ADVERTISING

Outdoor advertising is created at surprisingly low resolutions. Artwork is usually built to a scale of either ⅛", ¼", or ½" in the electronic file is equivalent to one foot in the printed output. The outdoor company will tell you which scale to use. Unfortunately, it isn't consistent from format to format or company to company. Resolution may also vary, depending in part on the technology being used to produce the final product. But the resolution usually cannot be more than 600ppi or less than 300ppi at the scale specified. Obviously, higher resolution will result in better-looking images.

There's an inconsistency in the way viewing sizes and mechanical sizes are given. It can be quite confusing and could lead to some costly mistakes. *Viewing* area is *always* specified with height first then width (unlike print advertising where width is always first, then height). I have never seen these dimensions listed differently. However, *mechanical* specifications can be inconsistent, sometimes listing width first, then height. Read specifications carefully, make sure you reconcile the viewing area dimensions and the mechanical dimensions. Don't hesitate to ask questions when in doubt. It's better to look inexperienced at the beginning than like a complete fool at the end.

The following specifications provide an idea of the various common outdoor formats used. The mechanical specifications are samples only. Unless otherwise specified, the resolution for all sizes should be 600ppi for best quality, but may be as low as 300ppi. Always check with your outdoor company to obtain their specs before starting a job.

Standard Bulletin
Viewing area: 14'h x 48'w
Mechanical specifications: ¼" = 1'
Bleed: 3.75"h x 12.25"w
Live: 3.5"h x 12"w

Premiere Square
Viewing area: 26'h x 24'w
Mechanical specifications: ¼" = 1'
Bleed: 6.75"h x 6.25"w
Live: 6.5"h x 6"w
Resolution: 600ppi

30-Sheet Poster
Viewing area: 10'5"h x 22'8"w (5.25"h x 11.75"w)
Mechanical specifications: ½" = 1'
Bleed: 5.75"h x 11.75"w
Live: 4.75"h x 10.75"w

Transit Shelter Poster (Bus Shelter) and Mall Kiosk (Note the H/W inconsistency)
Viewing area: 5.562"w x 8.187"h
Mechanical specifications: ⅛" = 1'
Bleed: 5.937"w x 8.562"h
Live: 5.5"w x 8.125"h

King-Size Bus Side Poster (Bus King)
Viewing area 30"h x 144"w
Mechanical specifications: ⅛" = 1'
Bleed: 30.5"h x 231" w
Live: 30"h x 230"w
Resolution: 300ppi

FIGURE 4-4

4. Open **Kick.tif**. It has been provided with a clipping path created by the folks at Photospin.com. Rename background layer *kick*, make a group with the same name and move the layer into the group. Open the Paths palette and load the clipping path as a selection. The image is quite small so add only a 1-pixel feather, then add a layer mask. The concept is to have her appear to be sitting on the frame of the billboard. The illusion will work better without the rear hand, so use the layer mask to conceal that hand (**FIGURE 4-4**). Save your document.

SET UP THE FINAL DOCUMENT

This will be a 14′ x 48′ billboard, and **outdoor advertising measurements are always given height first, then width**. The outdoor company provided these mechanical specs: ¼ inch = 1 foot. The preferred resolution at that size is 600 ppi, but you can go as low as 300 ppi. The color mode is CMYK. You need to allow ⅛ inch on all sides for bleed. So, if you were doing a normal 14 x 48 billboard, your document would be 3.75″ x 12.25″. However, you are going to add a four-foot extension on the top of the billboard. That makes the mechanical size 4.75″ x 12.25″. At 600 ppi this results in a document that is 74.2 MB. That's a fairly large document and by the time you finish the compositing and retouching it is going to be considerably larger. But, large as it is, it's still far smaller than one might expect, considering how large it will be printed.

For the other projects in this book I have cut the mechanical sizes in half to accommodate readers with less RAM or slower processors. However, a good portion of this project involves retouching and to really see how the tools work, you should do your retouching on higher resolution images. If possible, I would like you to work at the size specified. If RAM is an issue for you, go ahead and cut the resolution in half. You will need to lower the resolution for each image provided. Be sure to Save As to preserve your original images. In the workplace when document size and computer performance is an issue, it is not uncommon to do the retouching in separate documents, save those documents with all the layers for editing if necessary, then bring flattened versions into the final document. Personally, whenever possible, I prefer to have every-thing in one document. That makes it easier to do changes, and there are *always* changes.

1. Create a final document: 4.57″ x 12.25″ at 600ppi (or 300ppi), CMYK. Remember, outdoor measurements always specify the height first then the width. The new document dialog in Photoshop asks you to specify width first followed by height, so you will enter 12.25 in the first field and 4.57 in the second.

2. The manufacturer's specs list the live area as the same size as the trim. To quickly establish the live/trim area in your final document, make another document 3.5″ x 12″. Make the back-ground layer a dark color and drag it into your final document. Center it side to side and position it so the space at the bottom is equal to the space on the sides. The additional space at the top is for the extension. Drag guides to the edges of the new layer (**FIGURE 4-5**). After the guides are in place you can delete the reference layer. Save the document.

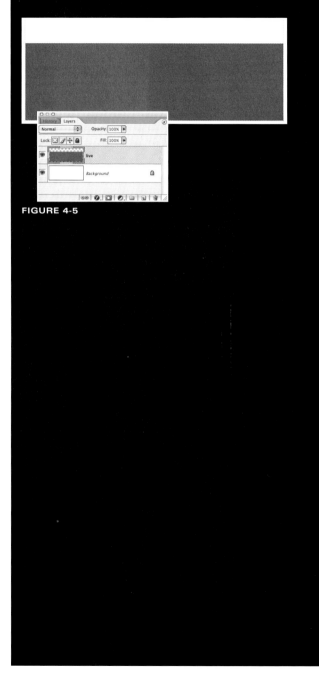

FIGURE 4-5

3. Drag the group KRISTIN from Kristin1.tif into P4.psd. Be sure the group KRISTIN is closed, then drag the group LEO from Leo.tif into P4.psd. Save and close Kristin1.tif.

4. Kristin is about the right size, but Leo is small in relation to her. Scale the group LEO to 120% and apply a Smart Sharpen filter to *leo*. Remember, whenever you upscale an image you are adding pixels (resampling). These extra pixels tend to soften the image. To compensate, you need to sharpen the image slightly. From the main menu choose Filter > Sharpen > Smart Sharpen. If you are working in CS, choose Unsharp Mask. Make the Amount 50 and Radius 1.5 and leave the other set-tings at their default values. In an ideal world you would never scale up, but the working world is far from ideal. You have to work with the images you are given. In Project 5 you will learn more about dealing with less-than-ideal assets.

5. Position the two so they are very close together, to help estab-lish their relationship. Place them to the far right to allow room for the show title and headline on the left—Western cultures

FIGURE 4-6

read left to right, so this positioning will help the ad track visually. Position Kristin so she appears to be looking at Leo and position Leo so his body is hiding the white strap on Kristin's shoulder. That small piece of strap is distracting. Place another guide ⅛″ from the top to accommodate bleed on Leo's hair. The top of Leo's head should just touch this guide (**FIGURE 4-6**).

Type and logos

You will be using Shape tools and Shape layers to create logos for the show and the network. If you're not up to speed on these tools, pause now to read **Photoshop Essential 4.1: Vector Masks, Shape Tools, and Shape Layers** at the end of this project.

FIGURE 4-7

1. Make a new group named *TYPE/LOGOS*. Select the Horizontal Type tool and choose a bold and slightly playful font. I chose Addled. The idea is to get something that will read easily from a distance, be heavy enough to allow us to incorporate the kicking figure, and have a somewhat comedic sensibility. Choose red, make the point size about 108.6. Type the word *MALE*. Position the word so it sits on the lower live area guide and touches the live area guide on the left. Set the tracking to about 60 (**FIGURE 4-7**).

FIGURE 4-8

2. Close the group TYPE/LOGOS and drag the group KICK from Kick.tif into P4.psd and close Kick.tif. Position Kick so her back appears to rest against the M in MALE. To make sure the MALE reads quickly it is necessary to increase the kerning between the M and the A to about 220. By opening it up you allow the viewer to see a portion of the A and hide less of the L with Kick's foot (**FIGURE 4-8**)

FIGURE 4-9

3. It is necessary to extend the letters of the show title so they bleed off the bottom and left sides. To do this you will convert the type into a shape, but to protect yourself, first duplicate the layer MALE so you have a copy in case you need to come back

and edit it later. Hide the original and highlight the copy. From the main menu choose Layer > Type > Convert to Shape. The letters have now become vector shapes, still resolution independent, but no longer editable as type (**FIGURE 4-9**).

4. Choose the Direct Selection tool and click on the bottom segment of the E. Press Shift and drag down to the bottom of the image window (**FIGURE 4-10**).

5. Repeat this for the L, the outsides of the M, and the other letters. For the center part of the M, do not press Shift, but click the individual points and drag each point to the bottom, maintaining the original angle of the M. Also drag the left side of the M to the left edge of the image window.

6. For the A do not use Shift, drag the bottom segment of each leg to the bottom of the image window while maintaining the letter's original angle. Kick will appear to be floating, but once the image is trimmed she will appear to be sitting on the frame of the billboard (**FIGURE 4-11**).

7. Choose the Type tool again, and type *ALPHA*. Make the point size about 43.5 and the tracking about 10. Use Transform to rotate the word making it look as if it has been kicked (**FIGURE 4-12**).

SET THE HEADLINE

Set the headline using Garamond bold to contrast the sans serif font used for the title. If you don't have Garamond, Times bold will work, too. Garamond is considered a friendly and highly legible font. Using sentence case also adds a friendly air. Be sure you have Smart Quotes activated, Preferences > Type > Smart Quotes (make sure it's checked). This will give you nice curly quote marks instead of daggers. Make the color black and the point size about 38. Set the tracking to 0. Tighten the kerning between the apostrophe and its neighboring letters. Since the copy refers to Leo, it should be placed near his face. Be careful not to put it right on live/trim, as this line will look better with a little room to breathe (**FIGURE 4-13**).

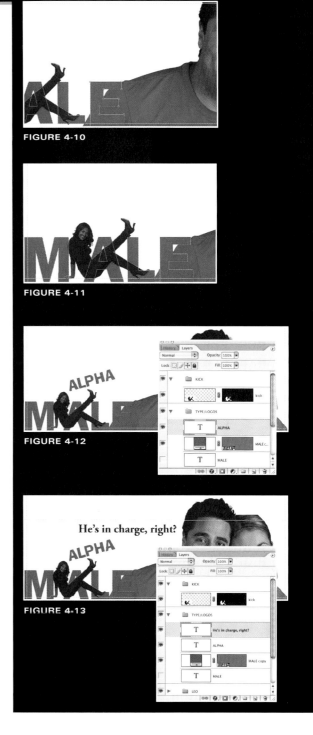

FIGURE 4-10

FIGURE 4-11

FIGURE 4-12

FIGURE 4-13

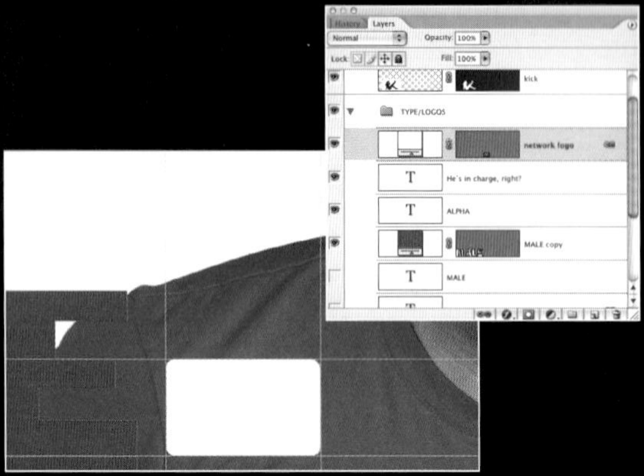

FIGURE 4-14

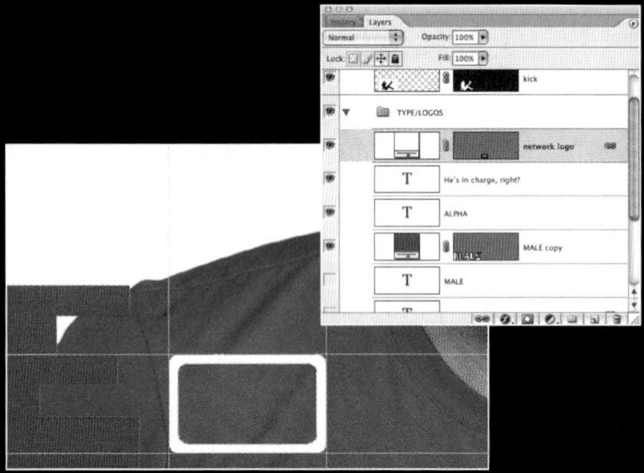

FIGURE 4-15

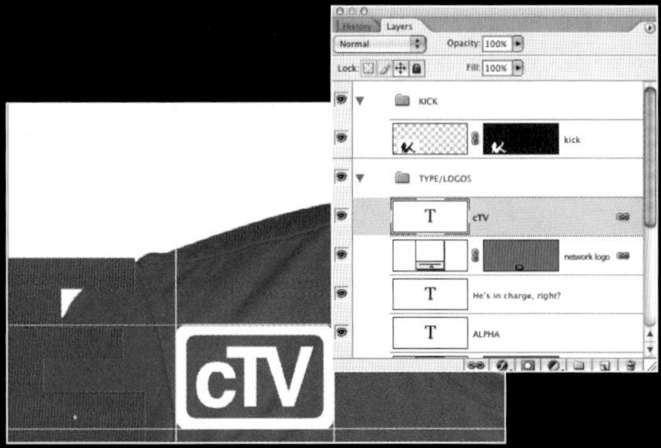

FIGURE 4-16

USE THE SHAPE TOOL
TO CREATE THE NETWORK LOGO

cTV is the network airing the new sitcom *Alpha Male*. A network would, of course, already have a logo. Since this is a fictional network you will create one using the Shape and Type tools.

1. Show Rulers, Command-R/Ctrl-R. Place a horizontal guide at the top of the center portion of the uppercase E in MALE and vertical guides at approximately 5.25″ and 6.5″. Make sure View > Snap To > Guides is checked.

2. Choose the Rounded Rectangle Tool from the assortment of Shape tools. Set the Radius to 50 px and white as the color. Create a rectangle shape using the horizontal guide you just placed as the top of the shape, the trim/live guide for the bottom, and the vertical guides just placed as the sides. This automatically creates a new Shape layer; name the layer *network logo* (**FIGURE 4-14**).

3. Choose *Exclude overlapping shape areas* from the Shape Area buttons in the options bar and create another, smaller rectangle inside the first one. Use the Path Selection tool [▶] to select both paths, then use the Align buttons [▦▦▦ ▦▦▦] [▦▦▦ ▦▦▦] to center the two rectangles. Use the Direct Selection arrow [▶] to select multiple points and the arrows on the keypad to adjust the width if necessary. Try to get a consistent width (**FIGURE 4-15**).

4. Select the Type tool and choose a bold sans serif font, such as Helvetica Bold, and type *cTV*. Tighten the kerning between the T and V so the letters touch and become a single unit. Also tighten the kerning between the c and T (**FIGURE 4-16**). The Type tool, typographic terms, and Layer styles are covered in detail in **Mini-Tutorial 3** at the end of Project 3.

5. With the Type tool, set *MON 7PM*. Again, use a bold font that can be easily read from a distance. I used DIN Black. To stack the type, press Return/Enter after MON and type 7PM. You will

need to tighten the tracking on MON and open the tracking on 7PM to justify the two lines (make them the same width). The leading should be fairly tight. The goal is to create a graphic block that is easy to read. Make the block the same height as the cTV logo. You can do this by highlighting the type and adjusting the point size and leading or by using the Transform command. The generally accepted rule is not to use more than 3 typefaces, preferably no more than two, in a single ad. I would argue that logos don't count as a typeface. I see them more as unique graphic elements.

6. To make the tune-in and logos "pop," that is, stand out from their surroundings, add glows from the Layer Style menu. With the layer MON 7PM highlighted, choose the Outer Glow effect from the Add Layer Style menu. Change the glow color to dark blue, the blending mode to Multiply, make the spread 9, and the size 12. Click the triangle at the right in the layer to show the effects that make up the layer style. Option/Alt-click the Effects bar and drag it down to cTV (make sure you press Option/Alt before clicking). Then, Option/Alt-drag the style to *network logo* (**FIGURE 4-17**).

7. Add a stroke to the Shape layer *MALE copy* to separate it from Leo's shirt. Select the layer and choose Stroke from the Add Layer Style menu. Make the size 21 and change the color to white (**FIGURE 4-18**).

Retouch the talent

Making people, especially entertainers and models in ads, look the best they possibly can while still appearing natural is one of Photoshop's greatest contributions to advertising and marketing. There are specific techniques that yield the best results, and there are tools that seem to work miracles. If you need a bit of brushing up, take time out to read **Photoshop Essential 4.2: The Retouching Tools**.

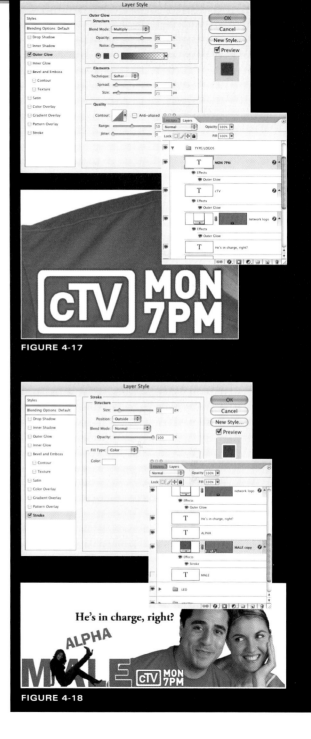

FIGURE 4-17

FIGURE 4-18

FIGURE 4-19

FIGURE 4-20

USE THE RETOUCHING TOOLS TO FIX THE TOP OF KRISTIN'S HEAD, GIVE HER A FRESHER LOOK, AND EVEN OUT HER MAKEUP

Unfortunately, in the image of Kristin1.tif the top of her head has been cropped off. We will need her full head, so this will have to be fixed. A few blemishes and wrinkles can be removed to give her a fresher appearance and there is a slight yellowish discoloration on part of her face that needs to be corrected.

When retouching, I find I get better results click, click, clicking with the mouse rather than dragging with either the mouse or the stylus. The retouching is more random this way, giving a more organic, less noticeable result. The brush size should be only slightly larger than the area being repaired.

Fix the top of the head

1. Make *kristin1* the active layer. Use the Lasso and make a selection around her existing hair just to the right of the part. Make sure the selected area includes some of the white background, so we get the outline of her head. Press Command-J/Ctrl-J. This copies the selected area and pastes it onto a new layer in exactly the same position. Use the Move tool to move it up to the top of her head. Because of the roundness of her head the hair in the back has a different curve from the chunk of hair we are using to extend the top of her head. To compensate, use Transform to rotate the copied hair about –9 degrees. Press Return/Enter or click the check mark in the options bar. Rename this layer *top of head* (**FIGURE 4-19**).

2. Turn off visibility for *top of head* temporarily and use the Pen tool to make a path outlining where the top of the head should be. Make *top of head* visible again, then load the path as a selection, add a 2-pixel feather and then click the *Add layer mask* button. With a brush, refine the mask adding a few irregularities to create a natural appearance (**FIGURE 4-20**).

RETOUCHING PEOPLE

Every image and every job is different with unique challenges and requirements, but a few generalizations can be made. Here are some things you need to do for almost every actor: remove "nuggets," small blemishes and imperfections such as pimples or acne scars. Reduce signs of age, including major wrinkles, crows feet, bags under the eyes, lines around the mouth and on the neck. Eyes and teeth nearly always need to be whitened. Sometimes the eyes need to be enlarged or widened to create a brighter, more alert look. You need to clean up and define facial hair, such as eyebrows, mustaches, and beards, and eliminate cross hairs (stray hairs from the top of the head that cross the forehead). When working on men, you want to make them look cleaner and well groomed without looking as if they just stepped out of a beauty salon. Often you will need to reduce the appearance of weight, remove double chins, and enhance the jawline.

How far to take all of this depends, in large part, on the attitude of the studio/network you are working for, the actors themselves, and the actors' "people." The biggest retouching mistake often made is overdoing it. It's easy to remove 5 years or so. Removing 20 with believable results is a challenge. Most places I work simply want the actors to look like a better version of themselves—rested, healthy, a little younger, perhaps a little thinner, but not completely transformed. Other places want the actors to be idealized versions of themselves with no wrinkles or imperfections whatsoever.

I once worked on the launch of a TV show that was a sequel to or rebirth of a popular show produced 20 years earlier. Several of the original cast members were returning for this production. This was a case where the network's marketing department wanted the actors to look very much as they did 20 years ago. Every time I presented a retouched image for approval, they said they wanted more work done. Essentially, they wanted all signs of age eliminated. That goes beyond retouching and becomes actual illustration. Not only is it a challenge to keep the person recognizable at that point, but the difference between the way they appear in print and they way the appear on screen can be startling. ■

3. The top of Kristin's head is not receiving much direct light, so the hair we copied from the rest of her head needs to be darkened with a Curves adjustment layer. Hold down Option/Alt and choose Curves from the Create new fill or adjustment layer menu. In the New Layer dialog, check the box labeled *Use Previous Layer to Create Clipping Mask*. In the Curves dialog, drag the right half of the curve upward to darken the layer until the pasted hair matches its surroundings (**FIGURE 4-21**).

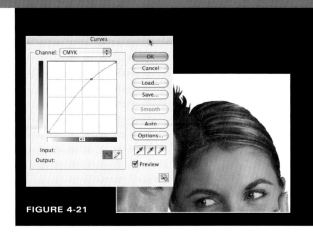

FIGURE 4-21

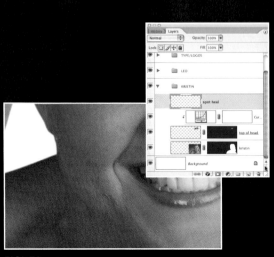

FIGURE 4-22

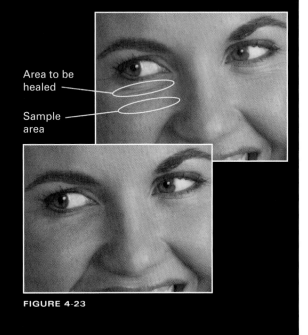

Area to be healed

Sample area

FIGURE 4-23

RETOUCH KRISTIN'S FACE

1. Make a new layer and name it *spot heal*. Choose the Spot Healing Brush tool. In the options bar, open the Brush Picker, make the brush diameter 30 and the hardness 50. Check *Sample All Layers*. Then, using several clicks, conceal the blemish on the left cheek (from your point of view). Perform the same steps on the strands of hair on her neck (**FIGURE 4-22**).

2. Make another new layer and name it *healing brush*. Choose the Healing Brush Tool. If you have a graphics tablet and stylus, this is a good place to use them, but the mouse will work fine, too. If you are using the stylus, make the diameter 30 pixels and the hardness 70. From the Size menu at the bottom of the Brush Picker, select *pen pressure*. If you are using the mouse, make the brush size just slightly larger than the width of the wrinkles you plan to repair (about 20 pixels should work). Unlike the Spot Healing Brush, to use the Healing Brush you need to sample an area that is blemish free. To make a sample, Option/Alt-click on a smooth place in the cheek area. Then draw over the wrinkles you wish to hide or *heal*. In this case, we're hiding the wrinkles under the eyes. Increase or reduce pressure on the stylus to keep the brush width as close as possible to the width of the wrinkle being repaired (**FIGURE 4-23**).

3. On the left (from your point of view) side of Kristin's face near her mouth is an area of yellow. To color correct it, use the Lasso to make a loose selection around the area. Add a 3-pixel feather, then add a Curves adjustment layer. Choose the yellow channel, add a point in the middle of the curve, and drag it down to reduce the amount of yellow. Go the magenta channel, add a point and move it up to increase the magenta, then click OK. Use a soft brush on a low flow setting to clean up the mask. Make sure the adjustment layer is only affecting the area that needs to be corrected (**FIGURE 4-24**).

4. Increase the overall contrast and punch up Kristin's layer group with a Levels adjustment layer (**FIGURE 4-25**).

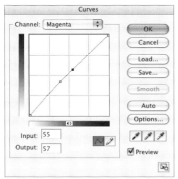

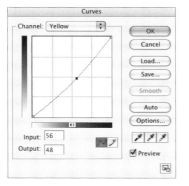

FIGURE 4-24

FIGURE 4-25

FIGURE 4-26

FIGURE 4-27

The retouching tools don't always produce the desired results. When they don't, the tried and true method of using a paint layer with an overlay grain layer will often do the trick. **Mini-Tutorial 4** (at the end of this project) walks you through this valuable technique.

RETOUCH LEO

The areas circled in red in **FIGURE 4-26** indicate the areas we need to fix. The blemishes need to be removed. Eyebrows need to be trimmed. Stray hairs on the forehead need to be removed. The beard stubble needs to be reduced and the jawline defined slightly. Also, there's a small amount of saliva in the corner of his mouth that needs to be eliminated.

1. On a new layer, use the Spot Healing Brush to fix small blemishes (**FIGURE 4-27**).

FIGURE 4-28

FIGURE 4-29

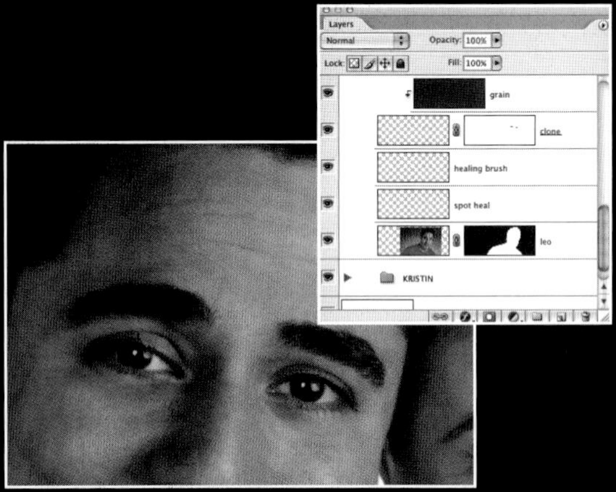

FIGURE 4-30

2. Make another layer and choose the Healing Brush. Use this tool to eliminate the stray hairs on his forehead and reduce the bags under his eyes (**FIGURE 4-28**).

3. The Healing Brush doesn't work well where there is strong contrast in hue and value in the target area. To clean up the eyebrows, use the Clone Stamp. Be sure to sample areas very close in value and hue to the area you are retouching. Use a brush of about 70 pixels in diameter and use the click, click method. Don't make the eyebrows too perfect. You don't want him to look as if he just stepped out of a beauty salon (even if he did). Use a layer mask to make corrections, bring back parts of the original eyebrow if you get carried away or lose control of the Clone Stamp tool (**FIGURE 4-29**).

4. If your cloning looks too blotchy, add a slight blur. But, when you add a blur, you almost always need to add a grain overlay layer to simulate the texture of the surrounding areas. This technique is explained in Mini-Tutorial 4 (**FIGURE 4-30**).

5. Use a paint layer with grain overlay layer to reduce the hot spots on Leo's face. Control the effect by lowering the layer opacity and use a layer mask to bring back a few selective highlights (**FIGURE 4-31**).

6. Use another paint with grain overlay to get rid of the saliva in the corner of his mouth (**FIGURE 4-32**).

FIGURE 4-31

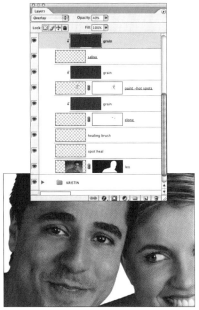

FIGURE 4-32

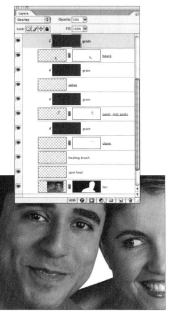

FIGURE 4-33

FIGURE 4-34

FIGURE 4-35

7. Reduce the stubble on his neck, above his upper lip, and add slight definition to his jawline with another paint layer and grain overlay layer (**FIGURE 4-33**). Right now his jaw just to the left of his chin tends to merge with his neck. Adding a slight highlight along the jaw in this area and smoothing out the color of the neck just below the jawline will help solve this problem. The highlight should be very subtle. Changing a person's jawline can radically change their appearance.

8. Color correct the yellow on his forehead by selecting the area, adding a feather, then adding a Curves adjustment layer (**FIGURE 4-34**).

9. Enhance the overall brightness and contrast with a Levels adjustment layer. Change the blending mode of the group LEO to Normal so the Levels adjustment layer won't affect KRISTIN (**FIGURE 4-35**).

FIGURE 4-36

FIGURE 4-37

FIGURE 4-38

FIGURE 4-36 is the before and after of Leo and Kristin. They have not been radically altered. They are simply fresher, brighter, more attractive versions of themselves. You would like people to think *"what a great picture of so and so,"* not *"so and so looks so different."*

PUT KRISTIN'S HEAD ON KICK'S BODY

Kick, the figure in the logo, is supposed to be our leading lady. Kristin was unavailable for a photo shoot so it will be necessary to put her head on the body of our double. This will require changing the skin color of the double to match Kristin's skin color.

1. Open **Kristin3.tif**. Highlight the *Background* and convert it to a regular layer by naming it *kristin3*. Use a layer mask to knock out everything except her head (**FIGURE 4-37**).

2. Drag the layer kristin3 into the KICK group in P4.psd. Close Kristin3.tif.

3. Lower the opacity of kristin3 to 70% so you can see Kick's head through Kristin's. Use Transform to reduce its size to 50% and press Return/Enter. Repeat this procedure once more. When making large changes in scale, you will get better results if you do it in stages (**FIGURE 4-38**).

4. After the second transformation, use Transform again to scale and tilt kristin3 so her eyes are at about the same angle and slightly larger than Kick's eyes, about 81%. Matching the eyes is usually a good way to get close to the right size. I usually make the layer I am reducing just a little larger. Head sizes vary and you will make the final transformation after you have brought the opacity back up to 100%. Making them a little larger gives you room to reduce more if necessary when you see the layer at 100% (**FIGURE 4-39**).

5. Hide *kristin3* temporarily. With the layer *kick* highlighted, press Option/Alt and add a Levels adjustment layer. Check *Use Previous Layer as a Clipping Mask* and click OK. Choose CMYK from

the Channel menu and lighten the image. Then, use the Pen tool to make a path around Kick's head. The point of this path is to remove the head, not preserve its outline. You don't need to carefully follow any of the details in the hair. But, you do need to pay attention to the neckline and the collar of the shirt. You will be replacing only the head, but it is important to preserve these elements in order to make the composite look believable. Load the path as a selection, add a 1-pixel feather and then, on the layer mask, fill the selection with black (**FIGURE 4-40**).

6. Show kristin3 and restore its opacity to 100%. Adjust the size and angle of her head, if necessary. It's better to have her head a little too big than a little too small, especially since this is a comedy. Working on kristin3 layer mask, reveal the back of the neck as necessary to make the head look anatomically correct on Kick's body (**FIGURE 4-41**).

7. To add to the top of Kristin's head, highlight kristin3 and use the Lasso to select a large chunk of hair. Press Command-J/Ctrl-J.

8. Move the new layer up to the top of the head and temporarily hide the layer. Use the Pen tool to make a path around what should be the top of the head. Load the path as a selection and add a 1-pixel feather. Show the copied hair layer and add a layer mask. On the mask blend the bottom edge of the copied hair layer into the original hair layer (**FIGURE 4-42**).

FIGURE 4-39

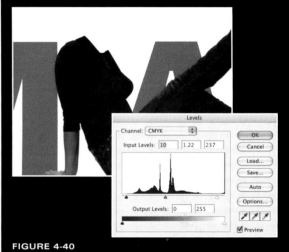

FIGURE 4-40

FIGURE 4-42

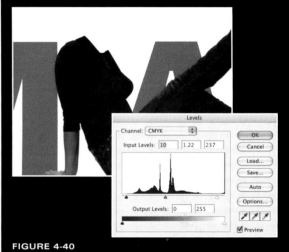

FIGURE 4-41

FIGURE 4-43

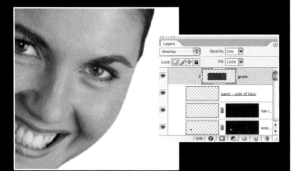

FIGURE 4-44

FIGURE 4-45

9. Command/Ctrl-click on *kristin3's* layer mask to load it as a selection. Add a new layer above *hair copy* and use paint with a grain overlay layer to fix the side of Kristin's face where her hand used to be (**FIGURE 4-43**). Since this image is very small, the noise will need to be reduced in size to get the right sized grain. I reduced it to 57%. When you reduce it this much, however, it no longer covers the paint area. You need to move the layer to the left until the grain appears over the paint. Then add a 1-pixel Gaussian blur. Lower the layer opacity of the grain layer to 50% or until it blends with the surrounding pixels (**FIGURE 4-44**).

10. Open **Kristin2.tif**. Use the Lasso to select the ponytail. Copy the ponytail and paste it into the KICK group. Drag the layer below the layer kick (**FIGURE 4-45**).

11. Use Transform to flip the ponytail and reduce it 50% twice. Use Transform again to rotate the ponytail (**FIGURE 4-46**).

12. Add a layer mask to ponytail, mask out the background, and shape the ponytail (**FIGURE 4-47**).

FIGURE 4-46

FIGURE 4-47

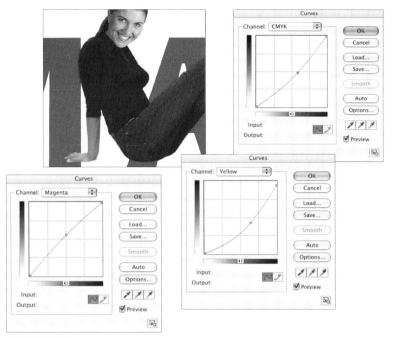

FIGURE 4-48

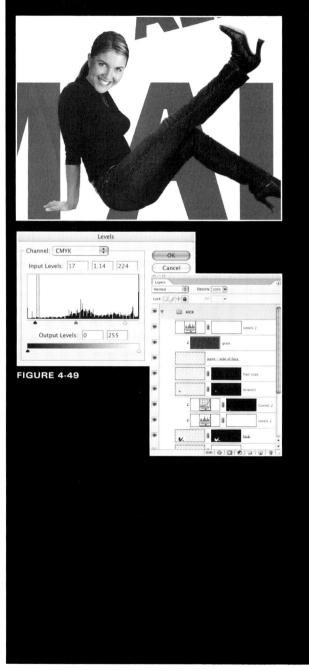

FIGURE 4-49

13. Kick's skin tone is too dark for Kristin's face. Make a loose selection around Kick's forearm. With the Levels adjustment layer above *kick* highlighted, Option/Alt-click *Add a new Curves adjustment layer, Use Previous Layer to Create Clipping Mask.* With CMYK chosen in the Channel menu lighten the skin tone, then go the yellow channel and reduce yellow, increase magenta in the magenta channel. Once the color is right, click OK then paint with white on the mask to reveal the adjustment layer on the bit of back that is showing and the part of the chest that is showing (**FIGURE 4-48**).

Finish up Kick

1. Increase the overall contrast and brightness with a Levels adjustment layer at the top of the KICK groups. Be sure to highlight group KICK and choose Normal on the Blending Modes menu (**FIGURE 4-49**).

2. Make a loose selection around the raised leg. Highlight the layer *Curves-skin* and add a new Curves adjustment layer above it, adding it to the clipping group with *kick* at its base. In CMYK, lighten the pants; choose the cyan channel and increase the cyan. Next increase magenta in the magenta channel. Try to get the color in the same hue range as Leo's shirt (**FIGURE 4-50**).

3. Clean up the boots. Select them, then use a Curves adjustment layer (also added to the *KICK* clipping group) to darken the boots. Then add a Solid Color layer to clean up the bottoms and edges of the boots, making sure to add it to the *KICK* clipping group. When the Color Picker is displayed, choose a dark gray and press OK. At first, the Color Fill layer will color the entire image area of *kick*. Fill the layer's mask with black to hide the effect, then reveal it on the soles of the boots using white. Change the blending mode to Multiply and lower the opacity to 70% to allow some of the texture and value of the boots to show through (**FIGURE 4-51**).

Since Leo and Kristin's heads extend beyond the top of the billboard, you may need to add bleed to the hair. Check with your outdoor company before doing this. Sometimes they prefer to handle the bleed on extensions themselves.

To help visualize what the billboard will look like on location, it is helpful to actually go out and photograph a billboard in town and replace the existing billboard with your own. If you can't find a photogenic location, get a good shot of a billboard, then shoot a location that appeals to you. Use Photoshop to create the ideal setting for your artwork (**FIGURE 4-52**).

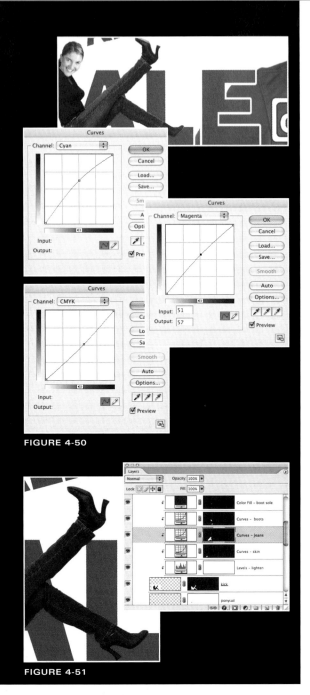

FIGURE 4-50

FIGURE 4-51

FIGURE 4-52

Adobe has integrated a number of vector-based tools and features into Photoshop. Since they are vector-based rather than pixel-based, they are resolution-independent and can be transformed without loss of quality. They are also editable. We have already used two of these tools, the Pen and Type tools, in previous projects. Now, let's take a look at vector masks, Shape tools, and Shape layers.

Vector Masks

Each layer can have a normal layer mask and/or a vector mask. By this time you are very familiar with normal layer masks. Vector masks, like normal layer masks, reveal or conceal the contents of a layer. Unlike normal masks, the areas that are revealed or concealed are defined by paths rather than by pixels. Because of this, vector masks do not support feathered edges, gradations, or blurs; they can have only hard edges. If you wish to have feathered edges or gradations, you have to use the vector masks in combination with layer masks.

You already know that to add a normal layer mask you can click the *Add layer mask* button at the bottom of the Layers palette. When a layer mask already exists, that button becomes the *Add vector mask* button. You can also add a vector mask by going to the main menu and choosing Layer > Vector Mask > Reveal All or Hide All. With the vector mask active (indicated by a frame around the vector mask in the Layers palette), use the Pen tool to make a path. If an existing path in the Paths palette is highlighted when a vector mask is added, that path will be applied to the vector mask (**PE 4.1A**).

Whether each path reveals or hides the contents of the layer is controlled by the Path Area button that is currently selected in the options bar. Don't worry if you have created a path with the wrong button selected, the path can be changed from one path area option to another by selecting the path using the Path Selection tool (black arrow) and then choosing another option from the Shape Area buttons (**PE 4.1B**).

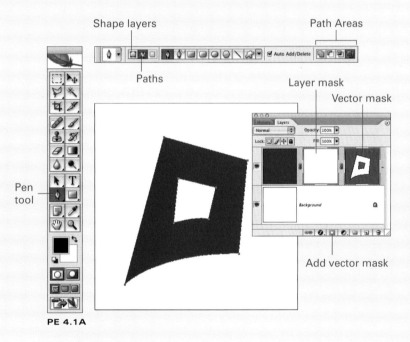

Shape layers

Paths

Path Areas

Layer mask

Vector mask

Pen tool

Add vector mask

PE 4.1A

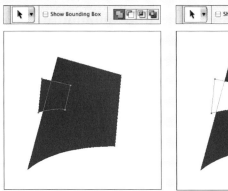
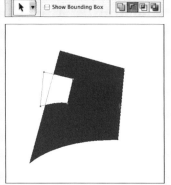
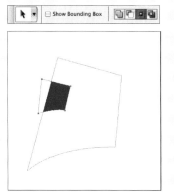
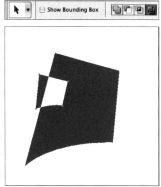

PE 4.1B

Shape layers

Custom Shape Picker

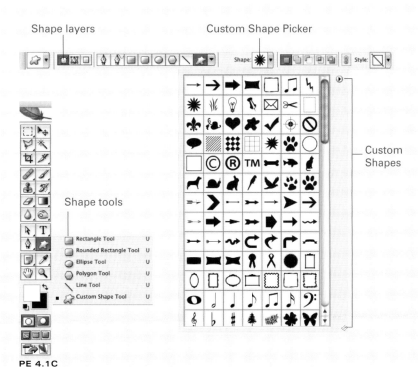

Custom Shapes

Shape tools

Rectangle Tool   U
Rounded Rectangle Tool   U
Ellipse Tool   U
Polygon Tool   U
Line Tool   U
Custom Shape Tool   U

PE 4.1C

Shape Tools and Shape Layers

Shape tools are used to create Shape layers, which are actually Fill layers with a vector mask containing a path. There are six Shape tools. The icons are good representations of the shapes that each will create, with the exception of the Custom Shape tool. The Custom Shape tool is not one single shape. Upon choosing it, the Custom Shapes Picker becomes available from the options bar, allowing you access to a large library of Shapes presets (**PE 4.1C**).

To make a Shape layer, select a Shape tool and click the Shape Layers button ▣ on the options bar. Choose a color by clicking the color swatch in the options bar and selecting a color from the Color Picker. Drag in the image window. A Shape layer is automatically added to the Layers palette. As with vector mask paths, the Shape Area buttons play an important role in creating shapes. When working in Shape Layers mode, there are five buttons to choose from ▣▣▣▣▣. If the first button is selected, every time you drag you create a new Shape

continues…

Create New Shape layer

Shape Area buttons

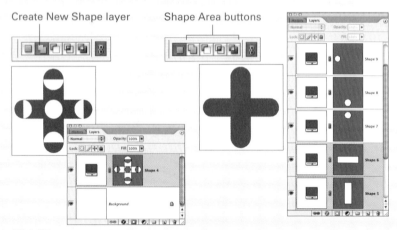

PE 4.1D

layer. With any of the other buttons, each time you drag you will modify the currently active Shape layer (**PE 4.1D**).

There are a couple of ways to make Shape layers without using the Shape tools. You have probably already created a Shape layer by mistake with the Pen tool. As with the Shape tool, the Pen tool has two mode choices in the options bar—Shape Layers and Paths. When you choose the Shape Layer mode and make a path a new Shape layer is automatically added to the Layers palette (**PE 4.1E**).

You can also convert a Type layer to a Shape layer. Be sure to duplicate the original Type layer first. Once it has been converted to a Shape layer, it is no longer editable type. To change a Type layer into a Shape layer, in the main menu go to Layer > Type > Convert to Shape. Once the type has been converted to a shape, you can use the Pen tools and the Direct Selection tool to edit the shape (**PE 4.1F**).

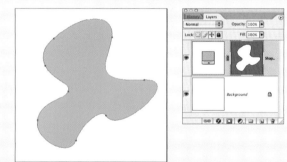

PE 4.1E

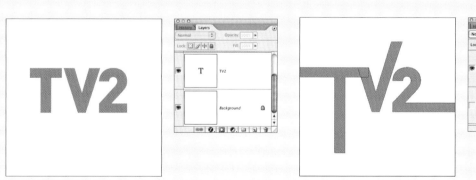

PE 4.1F

Change content

The content of Shape layers can easily be changed, opening up many creative possibilities. To change content, in the main menu go to Layer > Change Layer Content and choose one of the other Fill layer types (Gradient or Pattern) or change the layer into an adjustment layer (**PE 4.1G**).

Combine with Layer Styles and Layer Masks

When you choose a Shape tool, you can apply a Style preset when you first create the shape by selecting a style from the Style Picker in the options bar. You can add a style later by clicking the Layer Style button at the bottom of the Layers palette and choosing an effect from the menu. Shape layers can also have layer masks which you can use to create soft edges and opacity gradations (**PE 4.1H**).

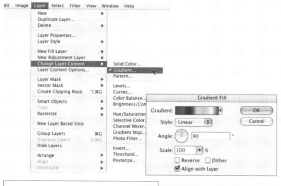

PE 4.1G

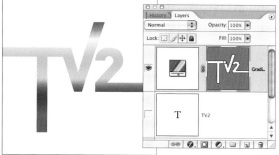

PE 4.1H

Before we had computers retouching was done with real airbrushes, using illustration board and acetate overlays. We taped a photographic print to the illustration board along with layers of specially coated acetate. The areas to be retouched were divided into major sections with an acetate overlay for each one. An airbrush and a variety of mostly home-made stencils were used to paint away blemishes and enhance the actor's appearance. This method was not only very toxic, it also resulted in an overly smooth, unnatural look. All the film grain and skin texture was eliminated along with the wrinkles. If a lot of retouching was required, the image ended up looking like an illustration and not like a photograph at all.

The reason it looked unnatural is that all images shot on film have film grain, all digital images have pixels, and people's skin has texture. For retouching to be completely believable, these textures needed to be preserved. Photoshop's retouching tools have been developed with this in mind. These tools seek to preserve both the texture of the skin and the integrity of the pixels.

The **Clone Stamp tool** used to be the primary tool for retouching. It works by sampling a "good" area (the source) and cloning that area on top of a "bad" area (the target) (**PE 4.2A**). The Clone Stamp uses the various brush tools to do its work. Option/Alt-click in the area you want to clone, then brush the cloned pixels over the spot that needs repairing. Because you're changing actual pixels, it's best to create a new layer above the original and make the repairs on the upper layer. Check *Sample All Layers* in the Clone Tool options bar to use the original layer as the source for your clone. It is generally best to use a soft brush so the edges blend with the surrounding pixels. A hard brush will create a clearly defined circle, but the soft brush blurs the pixels on its perimeter. For this reason you should use as small a brush as possible and do only as much as is really necessary. Overdone cloning can result in a mushy, overworked look, and the integrity of the pixels and textures can become completely compromised. The other problem with cloning is that it copies the source area exactly. You have to sample an area of the same hue and value for this technique to produce satisfactory results. Otherwise, the cloned area may stand out like a sore thumb (**PE 4.2B**).

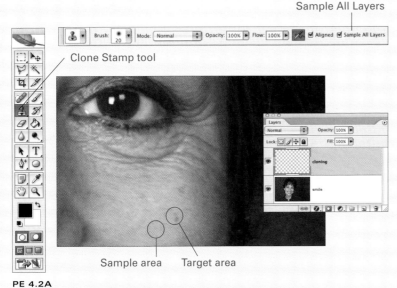

Sample All Layers

Clone Stamp tool

Sample area   Target area

PE 4.2A

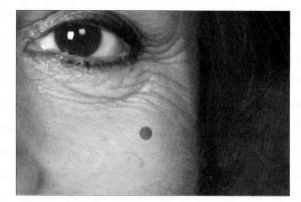

PE 4.2B

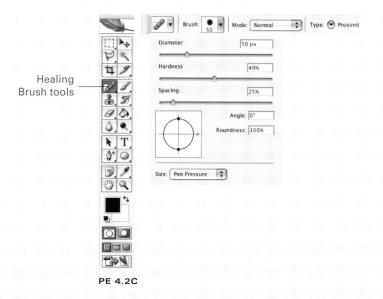

Healing Brush tools

PE 4.2C

Tip: When retouching I like to have both a mouse and stylus available. In many situations, I find that a click, move, click technique produces a more random, organic, and less obvious result. Other times I like to "draw" using the stylus. This works well when healing a wrinkle.

Photoshop CS2 provides us with four *healing* tools—the **Spot Healing Brush**, the **Healing Brush** tool, the **Patch** tool, and the **Red Eye** tool. With the two healing brush tools, the full range of Brush Presets is not available. In the Brush Picker you set the diameter, hardness, spacing, angle, and roundness. You can also choose whether you wish to have Pen Pressure or Stylus Wheel determine the brush size (**PE 4.2C**). Photoshop CS offers only the Healing Brush and Patch tool. Of these two, only the Patch tool requires you to work directly on the image—destructively. The Patch tool can produce impressive results, but if you use it, be sure to duplicate your original image first and work on the copied layer. Because of its destructive nature, I never use it and we won't spend time discussing it here—it's too important to be able to modify your retouching by reducing Layer opacity or changing Blending Modes. You can do this by using duplicate layers, but that can become cumbersome, and why bother when you can obtain just as good results other ways? The Red Eye tool doesn't work in CMYK, so we won't spend time on it here, either.

The **Spot Healing Brush** is great for small areas, sometimes referred to as nuggets. New to CS2, this is the first healing or cloning tool that doesn't require you to sample another area. You just click the spot you want to heal and the brush uses surrounding information to do its magic. Be sure to check Sample All Layers in the options bar, so you

continues…

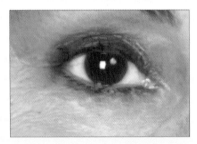

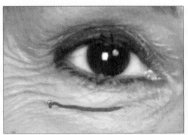
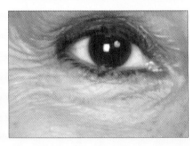

PE 4.2D

PE 4.2E

can work on a separate layer. The size should be slightly larger than the area you wish to heal; a soft brush will help it to blend with surrounding pixels, but too soft will result in mushy edges. Use this tool to heal the smaller blemishes. You can use this tool either with the mouse for spotting (correcting small blemishes with a series of clicks), or with the stylus for drawing over a winkle. Do not use it in areas with a lot of small wrinkles or of strong contrast in hue or value, which can produce a blotchy and muddy result (**PE 4.2D**).

The **Healing Brush** works by sampling one area and painting with those pixels over another area. Unlike the Clone Stamp, the Healing Brush maintains the color and lighting of the target area rather than replacing it with that from the source area. Be sure to work on a separate layer and check Sample All Layers in the options bar. Option/Alt-click an area you wish to sample, then move to the area you wish to correct (**PE 4.2E**). As with the Spot Healing Brush, areas of extreme contrast can be problematic.

For areas that are difficult to correct using these tools, using a paint layer with a grain overlay layer may be your best bet. See **Mini-Tutorial 4** for a step-by-step introduction to this technique.

Retouching using a paint layer with an overlay grain layer

The Healing tools are great when they work, but there are times when they just don't produce satisfactory results. In this tutorial you will learn one of my favorite techniques for retouching problem areas.

You will use paint to cover the undesirable area— this could be wrinkles, another model's body part that needs to be removed, unwanted hair or beard stubble, makeup that is too heavy or the wrong color, or skin tone variations. Then, to simulate the grain and skin texture, you will use a noise-filled layer, called the grain overlay layer, on the Blending Mode *Overlay*.

1. Open **Smile.tif**. Make a new layer named *paint*.

2. Choose the Brush tool and select a soft brush about 50 pixels in diameter. With the other re-touching tools you usually want to use a brush no larger than necessary to do the job. This technique works better if you use a bit larger bush at a brush opacity of about 50%.

3. Zoom in close. Press Option/Alt to access the eyedropper and sample the color under her eye near the area you wish to repair. As you work you will need to resample the image continu-ally so the color of your paint matches the hue and value of the surrounding pixels in the area you are repairing.

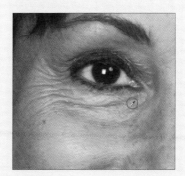

4. Do not drag, but rather click, click, click, over-lapping the sprays of paint and building up opacity gradually.

5. If the painting looks a bit blotchy, go to Filter > Blur > Gaussian Blur and blur the layer about 4 pixels.

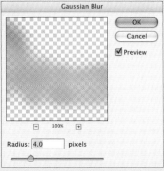

6. Option/Alt-click on the *Create new layer* button at the bottom of the Layers palette. In the dia-log check Use Previous Layer to Create Clipping Mask and from the Mode menu select Overlay. Once you have selected Overlay check Fill with Overlay-neutral color (50% gray) and click OK. A fill of 50% gray and a Blending Mode of Overlay can't be seen even though the layer is filled and 100% opaque. However, you can add effects to it and they will be seen.

7. Go to Filter > Noise > Add Noise. How much noise to add is a matter of trial and error. It is determined in part by the resolution of the image and the texture you are trying to match. Unfortunately, you won't know what it looks like until you press OK. For this image try 35% and choose Gaussian from the Distribution pane. Click OK.

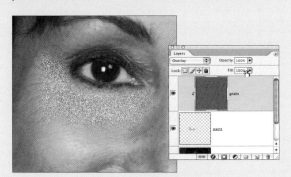

8. The Noise filter lets you add more or less noise, but it doesn't let you modify the size of the noise. In order to match the existing texture, you nearly always need to either enlarge or reduce the size of the noise to match the surrounding texture of the image. You can enlarge or reduce the entire noise layer with the Transform command. When working in close, the Transform handles are not available and it is handier to enter numbers in the scale fields of the options bar. Click the link between the width and height to maintain the aspect ratio. Enter 125% and click the check mark.

Tip: If you are scaling the noise up a considerable amount, be aware that this will extend that layer well beyond the frame of the image window. You won't see it, but it will be there, taking up RAM. In such cases, it may be better to select the only the area you need and scale that area.

9. Once you have the size of the noise about right, you need to blur the noise slightly to soften the pixels. This will help them blend with the rest of the image. Go to Filter > Blur > Gaussian and enter 1 pixel. The amount of blur necessary will vary depending on the resolution of the image.

10. Lower the layer opacity of the grain layer to about 37% and lower the layer opacity of the layer *paint* to about 81% to let some of the original image show through.

And to show how well you've done, here's a before and after comparison.

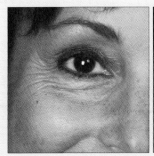

TRES MARIOS

CHALLENGE
FINAL

A
born
loser
with one
chance
to beat
the odds.

movie
MOVIE POSTER
poster

THE MOVIE POSTER IS ONE OF THE MOST CREATIVE, MOST

challenging jobs you can be given. It is the epitome of story-

telling. The goal is to tell the story and capture the emotion of

the 90-minute-or-more film in a single frame through the use

of imagery, color, typography, and artistic techniques. Guided

by an understanding of the audience, the genre, the medium,

and the marketing strategy, every decision in the creative pro-

cess is made with that goal in mind.

Several techniques common to movie posters are the use of contrast in scale and value and limited color palette. Limiting the color palette is a great way to unify disparate imagery and to make familiar or ordinary imagery look more artistic. Contrast is always a good way to attract attention and can be used to help tell the story. Often a large head or body will be combined with a vignette of a scene or element from the movie. This identifies the lead actor and helps inform the viewer about the nature of the film. Contrast in value is often used to create strong visual impact.

Before beginning a job such as this, you need to know what the movie is about and the intended audience. Often the actual film will not yet have been completed and you will be given a synopsis of the story. Along with the synopsis you may be given a creative brief that will tell you who the audience is and the strategic thinking of the marketing department.

Here is the information for this movie. I made up the story, based largely on the imagery I had available.

title   *Final Challenge.* This is the third and final installment of the *Challenge* series of films.

audience   Males 18 to 34.

synopsis   This is the story of a young male immigrant who has been mistakenly identified as a terrorist and is being aggressively hunted by special military agents. Though very bright, he is uneducated and speaks broken English. The only thing he knows how to do is fight. In the back streets and seedy boxing rings of border towns he becomes known for his ability to pound the daylights out of his opponents in record time. He is not proud of this talent, but must exploit it in order to survive. He meets and falls in love with a beautiful Malaysian woman who is indentured to the smuggler who brought her into the United States. She becomes pregnant with the fighter's child. He wants to leave the violent and dark life he has come to know and make a better one for himself, the woman he loves, and their baby. But first he must buy her freedom. He will need more money than he has ever even dreamed of. There is only one way to get it—go to the big city for a boxing match with the reigning champion. A win would mean a new life. It would also mean coming out of hiding at the risk of losing everything.

ASSETS

For this poster you have been provided with a near-full-body shot of the lead male actor, Tres Marios, and a headshot of the female lead. You'll tell the story by combining these images with stock photography.

You'll use all the tools and techniques from Projects 1 through 4, and add these:

- ✔ Channel Mixer
- ✔ Layer Fill
- ✔ Posterizing
- ✔ Rescaling (Enlarging)

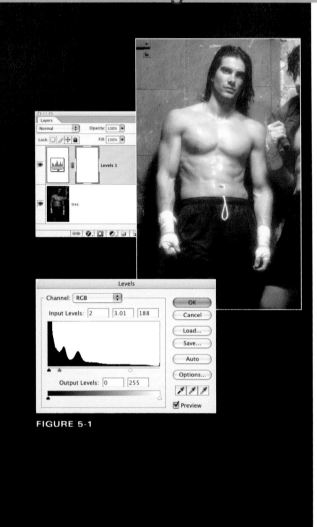

FIGURE 5-1

Set the stage

This project is the culmination of everything you have learned in the previous four projects. Virtually every technique and tool used so far will be used here. You will build this project in much the same way as you would a real job— moving back and forth between elements, enhancing and refining the composite as you go. Real jobs are not linear, as most tutorials are—they evolve, one thing leading to another. That is how you will work in the project.

KNOCK OUT THE BACKGROUNDS

Posters can be broadly classified as *star sell*, *story sell*, or *big concept*. In fact, they are often combinations of these. This poster is largely a star sell. As mentioned earlier, we want to reinforce Tres' branding as a tough, sexy, leading man. But in order to communicate with our target audience, we also need to emphasize the story. We are featuring Tres Marios, the actor, by having him front and center, but he is *in character*, as though he has just come off the set. When discussing a movie, it is easy to confuse the actor and the character. For the purpose of this project, we'll be referring to Tres, the actor rather than the character. The actor who plays Yasmin is secondary to her character, so we'll be referring to Yasmin the character, rather than the actor.

1. First you will prepare the actors' images by knocking out their backgrounds using layer masks.

2. Open **Tres.tif**. Rename the Background *tres*. You'll use the Pen tool to make a path around Tres. But the image is very dark and in places it is hard to determine where the path should be. To help you see what's going on add a Levels adjustment layer. Lighten the image by moving the middle triangle to the left; don't worry about how it makes the image look, only about seeing the details in the shadows. This makes the image look very bad, but this layer is only there to help you create the path and will be discarded later. Even with it lightened there will be places lacking information and you will need to guess (**FIGURE 5-1**).

BE PREPARED TO "SELL" YOUR DESIGN

Very often the people with the authority to approve your design are not visually oriented. They spend much of their time thinking about budgets and ways to increase market share. Words and deductive reasoning are their tools of comfort. Many times they really can't tell whether a design is good or bad. Often they need and want to be convinced. Whether your work is the product of deep thought or pure gut-level creativity, you have to be prepared to sell your design with words, assuring the executives it has merit and supports their marketing strategy—and is the perfect solution to their problem.

Here is my rationale for this poster. It is an example of how you may need to defend and promote your design.

This poster tells the story with passion and intensity. It speaks to the target audience through the use of color, imagery, and artistic technique. Enough of the story is told to pique interest, but not to give too much away. The images are not only literal elements from the movie, they are also representative of the drama and emotions being played out. The chain-link fence represents a harsh, lower-income urban environment and the tensions that exist there, but also symbolizes the barriers keeping Tres and Yasmin apart. The desert represents the terrain of the American Southwest where Tres hides out, but also symbolizes his struggle to triumph over harsh conditions. The running figure represents Tres being chased by military agents who suspect him of being a terrorist. It also symbolizes fear, desperation, and escape from his previous life—running to meet his destiny and the possibility of a new life: *hope*. The city

represents that destiny and all it entails—hope, confrontation, *challenge*. The sun behind Tres' head lends him a heroic, almost saintly quality and the contrast focuses attention squarely on him.

The look and feel are consistent with the established CHALLENGE franchise brand—strong warm color, dramatic imagery, bold typography, and high contrast. All of these speak to the target audience, males 18–34, creating a sense of masculine intensity, the challenge of a fight, danger, and triumph. The emotional impact, urban environment and sexual overtones are elements to which this audience will relate and find attractive.

Tres Marios, the lead actor, is prominently featured. He is presented as sexy and powerful. This reinforces his brand as an actor, adding to audience perception of him as a leading character in action/dramatic roles.

Compositionally, the viewer's eye is drawn into the picture and attention focuses on Tres' head. It is said the eyes are the window to the soul. Every element in the composition guides the viewer to Tres' eyes, Yasmin's gaze, the angle of the fence. the angle of the buildings, the light source behind Tres, the dark outside edges. All the elements, including typography, are integrated presenting a cohesive and strong message. Nothing looks like an afterthought or "stuck on." The color, transparent quality, arrangement of elements, the headline behind the head, the body copy relating to the curve of the arm, the light source, unite everything into a single, impactful statement. ■

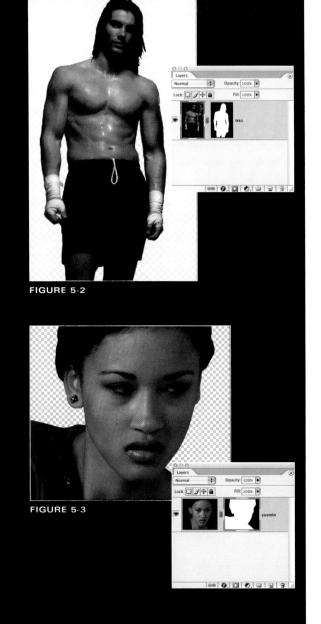

FIGURE 5-2

FIGURE 5-3

3. Use the Pen tool to make a path around Tres. Pay special attention to his hair. Don't go nuts trying to get every hair, but do try to get the major chunks of hair, bumps, and curves. Later in the project you will refine the mask on the hair and make it more natural. Also, zoom in close and follow carefully the curves of his anatomy—paying attention to details will really pay off in the long run. The resulting composite will look much more natural and professional. You'll need to fake the area on the right upper arm that is covered by the other boxer's hand. You will fix this area later. Refer to the arm on the other side to get the anatomy right. When you are happy with the path, load it as a selection, add a feather, and then add a layer mask. Discard the Levels adjustment layer (**FIGURE 5-2**).

4. Open **Yasmin.tif**. Rename the Background *yasmin*. Make a path around her head and shoulders, add 1-pixel feather and a layer mask (**FIGURE 5-3**).

5. Save your documents. If RAM is an issue, close the documents for the time being. If not, leave them open and proceed to the next step.

SET UP THE FINAL DOCUMENT, START THE BACKGROUND, AND BRING IN THE MAIN CHARACTERS

Posters come in many sizes. One of the most common is 27″ x 40″ (add .25″ on all sides for bleed). They are typically created at 300ppi or higher. In CMYK, that results in a file of over 370MB—without layers. It's not uncommon to have a final document that is 1GB or more. To keep our document a more manageable size, we will make it half size at half the normal resolution. However, the final layered file will still be quite large—around 650MB. You may reduce the size further if you have limited RAM or disk space. Bear in mind that you will need to increase the percentages for transformations (scaling) of the source files to account for the reduction in size of the final document. This is necessary because source files and final documents are usually of different (ppi) resolutions.

Tip: To free up RAM you need to Purge from time to time. This will erase everything on the clipboard and in the History. History requires huge amounts of RAM. Choose Edit > Purge > All. You can also use the Crop tool at various stages to remove excess pixels that extend beyond the image window. This is destructive, however, and not recommended unless file size becomes a real problem.

Make a new document 13.75″ x 20.25″, 150ppi, CMYK, and save it as P5.psd. The live area is 12.5″ x 19″. To quickly establish the live area, create a new document that size. Fill the first layer with a dark color, hold Shift and drag that layer into P5.psd. Choose View > Snap, then choose View > Rulers (Command-R/Ctrl-R). Drag guides to the edges of the live reference layer (**FIGURE 5-4**). Once the guides are in place, discard the layer and uncheck Snap.

Before bringing in the main characters and other elements, let's set the stage a bit by bringing in the sky elements. This will establish the tone for the rest of the poster.

1. Make a new group in P5.psd named CITY/SKY. Open **Sky2.tif**, rename the Background *sky2* and drag it into CITY/SKY. Open **Sky1.tif**, rename its Background *sky1* and drag it into CITY/SKY. Duplicate *sky1* (Command-J/Ctrl-J). Then, activate the Free Transform command (Command-T/Ctrl-T), Control/right-click inside the transform area, and choose Flip Horizontal from the contextual menu. Press Return/Enter or click the checkmark on the options bar to commit the transformation (**FIGURE 5-5**). The guides can be hidden for the time being.

2. Position *sky1* and *sky1 copy* so the suns meet in the center, forming a sort of nuclear explosion. This creates a strong light source that will be directly behind our lead actor's head. Position *sky2* so the sun is just left of center (it will be hidden in the

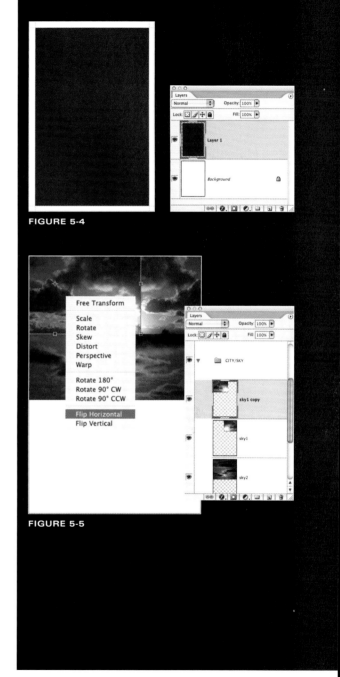

FIGURE 5-4

FIGURE 5-5

IT'S NOT AN IDEAL WORLD

In an ideal world, films would be completed before the marketing begins. Actors would gladly make themselves available for photo shoots whenever you need them. And all images would be of sufficient dimension and resolution that they would never have to be scaled up. Of course, it's not an ideal world. Marketing usually begins long before a film is finished. You may not have any images from the actual film to work with. The actors may be on location, and be unavailable or be unwilling to show up for a photo shoot. If they do show up, it is often under duress and they want to be done with it as soon as possible. They definitely won't be back for revisions. If there *is* a photo shoot, you probably won't be invited or consulted. More likely, you will be given a stack of contact sheets after the fact and be told this is all that is available. You'll have to make do with what you find there and combine it with stock photography. Many of the hard and fast rules you have been taught about never scaling an image up (enlarging) go right out the window. The following true story illustrates my point.

I was working on an outdoor campaign for the launch of a new television police drama. The campaign was already in full swing when the network decided to add another billboard to the mix. This one was to feature four members of the cast. The design was simple—big heads all in a row against a black background. As an addendum to the existing campaign, this billboard had to carry the same look and feel (branding) as the currently approved key art. That key art featured the head of the lead actor very dramatically lit, extremely warm in color and with a fairly heavy grainy overlay. That same image would be in the number one position (far left) on the billboard I was creating. The other actors' heads lining up next to it would have to have the same dramatic lighting, warm color, and grainy texture. No problem. I thought.

In addition to the lead actor, there was an African-American woman, a Hispanic man, and a Caucasian woman. The African-American and Hispanic were detectives, the Caucasian was a street cop. I was given a stack of 4 x 5 transparencies from which to choose my images. I found great photos of the two detectives. The quality and resolution were so good they would have to be degraded in order to match the existing key art. But again, I thought—no problem. I found only one decent shot of the street cop and she looked great, but nothing like a cop. She was dressed in a bright red cocktail dress. Her hair and makeup made her look very glamorous. I knew she would look out of place, but it was all had, and I proceeded to produce the artwork. It was tricky getting the other cast members to match the lead actor, but in the end it worked out OK. That is, until the president of the network saw it. His point of view was that although this ad was intended in part to build audience recognition of the other actors, it was primarily a branding ad for the show. That meant the actors had to appear in character and the street cop was definitely not in character. She needed to be in uniform and with little or no makeup.

I went back to the point person for photos and asked for everything he had of her in uniform. The only shot he could find was a 35mm full body. That meant her head was less than a quarter-inch high. On the billboard it had to be about six feet high! There was no time or budget for a new photo shoot. There was no choice but to make that one work.

I had the slide scanned at 600% at 600ppi. Two things happen when an image is enlarged that much: It picks up contrast and it loses detail. Actually, when the original is so small, the detail isn't there to begin with and you have to create it. Eventually, I got her to the point that she looked pretty good and from a distance you would never know her photo was of such different quality than the others.

If you are given assets that have already been scanned and they must be enlarged, here are a couple of tips. Scale up in stages. I usually go 150% at a time, but some people I know use increments of 110%. After you finish scaling, sharpen the image with the Unsharp Mask filter or CS2's new Smart Sharpen filter. Use these filters judiciously, because oversharpening results in an unnatural, pixelated look.

Specialty applications and third party filters are available that are reputed to do a good job of "rezzing–up" (up-scaling). I have not used them and can't vouch for their effectiveness. However, one that my students have given high marks is Genuine Fractals from Lizardtech. com. ■

final document) so the overall illumination in the layer is consistent with the position of the sun in *sky1*. The bottom of *sky2* should be slightly below the center of the document. The purpose of this layer is to fill in blank areas behind the buildings not covered by *sky1* and *sky1 copy*. Add layer masks to *sky1* and *sky1 copy*. Use a soft brush about 150 pixels in diameter, check airbrush, and set the flow at 50%. Use an irregular stroke to soften the edges of the two *sky1* layers and blend them with *sky2* below (**FIGURE 5-6**).

3. Close Sky1.tif and Sky2.tif. Save your final document.

Bring in the main characters

1. Make a new group in P5.psd named TRES. Drag the layer *tres* from Tres.tif into the new group. To really feature our leading man, Tres, and give him more presence, his image needs to be larger—about three-quarters as high as the overall image. Use Free Transform and scale *tres* 110% **three** times. Drag him to the center of the image (**FIGURE 5-7**).

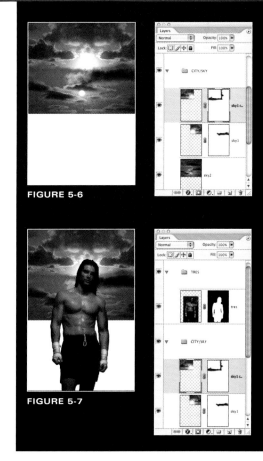

FIGURE 5-6

FIGURE 5-7

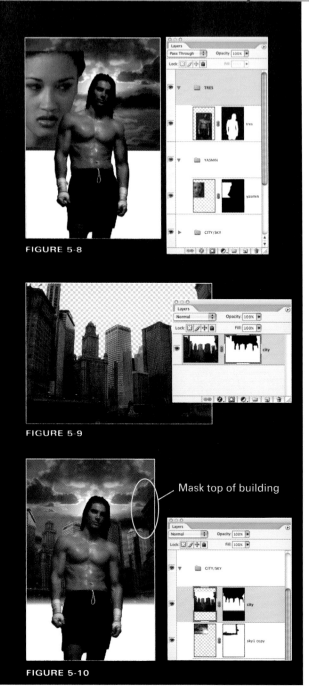

FIGURE 5-8

FIGURE 5-9

Mask top of building

FIGURE 5-10

2. Make a new group named YASMIN between CITY/SKY and TRES in P5.psd. Drag the layer *yasmin* from Yasmin.tif into the new group. Scale YASMIN to about 75% so her eyes are within the image frame but her face is slightly behind Tres. The show title will overlap her head but should not conceal her eyes, so place her so that her eyes are about 4.25″ from the top of the image window. (**FIGURE 5-8**). Save your document.

Colorize and unify

1. Open **City.tif** and rename the Background *city*. Choose the Magic Wand, set the Tolerance (in the options bar) to 32, and select the sky. Hold Shift to select the small area on the left and areas on the right that are gray rather than 100% white. Expand the selection 2 pixels (Select > Modify > Expand), add a 1-pixel feather, hold Option/Alt and add a layer mask. (**FIGURE 5-9**).

2. Back in the main document, hide the group YASMIN temporarily. Drag *city* into the group CITY/SKY and place it at the top of the stack in that group.

3. Scale the city to 70% so it doesn't dwarf our lead actor. Position *city* so the vanishing point of the perspective of the buildings is behind Tres and the buildings directly behind Tres are roughly level with his eyes.

4. Look closely at the top edge of *city*. You may see a line across the top of the layer. This often happens when bringing a masked layer into a larger document. When the selection was made and feathered in City.tif, one pixel across the top of the image was not selected as the mask was added. Use a brush at 100% opacity/flow and paint with black on the layer mask of *city* in P5.psd to clean this up. This is a good place to use the click-shift-click technique discussed way back in Project 1. Or, make a selection slightly larger than the line using the Rectangular Marquee tool and then fill the selection with black (be sure you're working on the mask and not the image). Also, the building on the right is cut off. Use the Lasso to select the top

section of the building above the top ledge and mask it so it appears that the ledge is the top of the building (**FIGURE 5-10**). Close City.tif. No need to save it.

5. To modify the color of the city and make it appear to be illuminated by the golden sky, hold Option/Alt and add a Solid Color fill layer by choosing Solid Color from the fill/adjustment layer menu at the bottom of the Layers palette. Check Use Previous Layer to Create Clipping Mask and click OK. When the Color Picker appears, use the cursor to select a golden orange from the sky. Increase the saturation in the Color Picker by raising the value of the S field (in HSB). (The result should be something like C=0, M=58, Y=96, K=0). Click OK and change the Layer blending mode to Color. The buildings now take on the golden glow of the sky (**FIGURE 5-11**).

6. Next, add a dark brown gradient layer to eliminate the white in the lower half and disguise the lower edge of the city photograph. Add a new layer above the fill layer and name it *dark brown*. Use the eyedropper tool to sample a dark brown color from the city. Choose the gradient tool, select Linear Gradient in the options bar and Foreground to Transparent from the presets. To ensure that the bottom edge of *city* is completely covered, **start slightly above** *city*'s lower edge, hold Shift, and make a short drag upward (about ¾ inch) to create a gradient on the bottom of the image (**FIGURE 5-12**).

7. A red Solid Color fill layer will help to unify the composite and provide a lighter background for Yasmin, and other elements such as the fence and desert that will be created later. With *dark brown* highlighted, add another Solid Color fill. Choose red as the color. Add the word *red* after *Color Fill* in the Layers palette to distinguish it from the previous Color Fill layer. Fill the mask on the layer with black to completely hide the layer, then use white with a large (800-pixel) soft airbrush on a flow of 40% to gradually reveal the red around the outer portions of the image area. Leave an egg-shaped transparent area in the center and upper right. Reduce the Layer opacity to 76% (**FIGURE 5-13**).

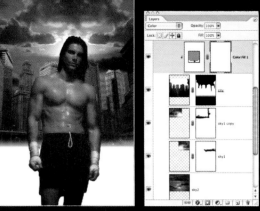

FIGURE 5-11

Direction and length of drag

FIGURE 5-12

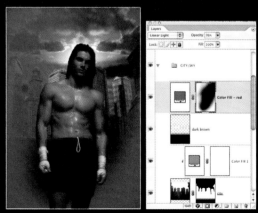

FIGURE 5-13

STOCK PHOTOGRAPHY

Once you are clear on what type of composite you are creating, you have to decide what specific types of images you want and where you are going to get them. Some of the images for the ad may be provided by the client. The rest you will have to obtain yourself. This means either you hire a professional photographer (usually very expensive), shoot the images yourself (not as tough as it sounds), or turn to stock photography (usually the easiest solution). If you hire a photographer you need to have a contract with the photographer specifying who owns the copyright for the images. Likewise, if you shoot the photographs yourself and you are working for someone else, it needs to be clear who owns the copyright. Many agencies and studios require you to sign a contract that says they own the copyright on everything you create for the job. Stock photographs are images you can license from companies that maintain large photo libraries. These companies have contracts with the photographers that allow them to grant copyright privileges to others for a fee and under certain conditions. These companies and their resources can be accessed online. Their websites utilize the best available search engines, making the job of finding images easier than it has ever been. If you were doing an ad for a thriller movie, you could type *fear* in the keyword field and the search engine would instantly retrieve all the images that might express that emotion.

The two types of stock photographs are *rights managed* and *royalty free*. Every time you use a rights managed image you pay a fee and the photographer is paid a royalty. The fee gives you the right to use that image for a specific purpose and time. For example, you might buy the right to use the image in the June issue of *People* magazine. If you or your client wants to use the image again, say in September, you will have to pay for it again. This can get very expensive since most rights managed photos start at around $1500. The actual amount is determined by where and how it will be used, how many times it will be used, and how important the image will be to the overall design. There is no exact formula and most of these contracts are highly negotiable. It is important to know ahead of time all the ways the image will be used so you can negotiate the best deal right at the beginning. If you come back later, after an ad has already run, and tell the stock photo company you want to run the same ad again in a different issue or different magazine, you have very little negotiating power. You must make it clear to your clients up front that they pay for the right to use the image only as specified in the agreement you have made with the stock photo house. If you want to use it any way other than what was specified, the client will incur additional charges. Many clients do not understand this and will likely be very unhappy if you inform them of it after the fact.

Royalty free images, on the other hand, may be licensed for multiple uses in multiple media without incurring extra charges. You pay for the image or collection of images once, and then you can use them as many times as you like. Also, royalty free images are generally much less expensive than rights managed ones. There are often some restrictions, though, on how the images can be used. For example, most can't be used in association with pornographic material and you can't use the image of a person in such a way that he or she appears to be endorsing a particular product or service. There may be other restrictions; you should read the licensing agreement and then speak with a sales representative if you have questions.

If royalty free images are less expensive and can be used multiple times, why use rights managed images at all? **Selection** may be one reason, **exclusivity** another. Royalty free images used to be very generic. They had to be because they were intended to appeal to the widest audience possible. If you wanted something unusual or unique, you had to use rights managed. But today, royalty free stock photography is a huge business and the number of royalty free images available is certainly in the hundreds of thousands, if not millions. The search engines make it easy to sift through them to find exactly what you are looking for. However, if you find a really great and unusual image, chances are someone else has found it, too. That means there is the possibility two people may end up using the same image in the same issue of the same publication. This nearly happened to me. I once created a series of ads for a cable network using royalty free images. For one of the ads I used a great image of a woman in dark glasses with her hands stretched out toward the camera. It was shot from a high angle and was very dramatic—perfect for

my concept. The ad was going to run in a cable industry trade publication. At the last minute the client decided to run one of the other ads I created. When that magazine came out, there was an ad by a competitor that featured the very same image of the woman I had used in the ad that didn't run. Had it been a rights managed image that would have been less likely to happen. You license a rights managed image for a specific period of time for use in a specific category of publications. In effect, you buy the exclusive right to use that image for the length of your license agreement. The catch is, while you have exclusive rights to that image, there may be other images, even using the same model, that are extremely similar. The rep at the stock photo house should know this. Be sure to ask, as they may not volunteer this information on their own. Also, make sure any images of people have been model released. That means every person in the shot has signed a release saying their image may be used for commercial purposes. ■

8. Add a layer above *Color Fill - red* and name it *sun glow*. Choose a deep yellow (something like C=0, M=22, Y=74, K=0) for the foreground color. Choose the Gradient tool, select Radial Gradient, and Foreground to Transparent. Start behind Tres' head and drag about 3 inches. Since you are using a Radial Gradient, it doesn't matter which direction you drag, the result will be the same. Change the blending mode to Overlay (**FIGURE 5-14**).

Direction and length of drag

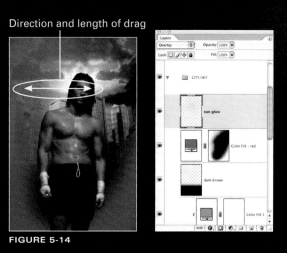

FIGURE 5-14

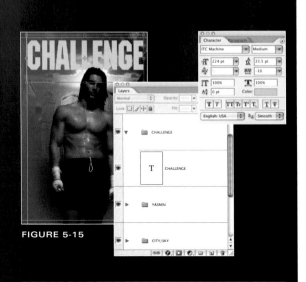

FIGURE 5-15

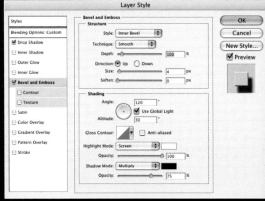

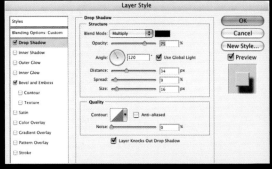

FIGURE 5-16

Title treatment

1. Make a new group named CHALLENGE. Place it between the groups TRES and YASMIN. Choose the Horizontal Type tool. Select a bold sans serif font such as ITC Machine. If you are using Machine, make the point size about 224 and tighten the tracking to about −10. If you are using another font, 224 points may cause your type to be far out of frame. Don't worry, you will use Free Transform to correct this. Choose a color that is easy to see. If your guides are not already showing, press Command-; /Ctrl-; (semicolon) to show them. Type *CHALLENGE*. Use the Free Transform command to distort and position the type. The idea is to have Tres' head partially covering the type on the bottom and have the sides extend nearly to the limit of the live area. Leave a little space on top for the star's name (**FIGURE 5-15**).

2. From the layer style menu at the bottom of the Layers palette choose Bevel and Emboss. For Style choose Inner Bevel, for Technique choose Smooth. Make the Depth 100%, the Size 4 pixels, Soften 0 pixels. In the Shading pane, set the opacity of Highlight to 100% and Shadow to 75%. Leave the other parameters at their default settings (**FIGURE 5-16**).

3. Before closing the Layer Style dialog, choose Drop Shadow, set the parameters as shown, and click OK. Reduce the Fill to 0% (located below Opacity in the Layers palette) (**FIGURE 5-17**).

4. Add a new layer above the type layer and name it *challenge hi lites*. With the new layer still highlighted, Command/Ctrl-click on the *CHALLENGE* type layer thumbnail to load the type as a selection, then add a layer mask to *challenge hi lites*. You will use this layer to paint highlights on the type, defining the edges so it is legible while remaining transparent. Usually I would use the Clipping Mask feature rather than a layer mask for this step, but because the layer fill has been reduced to 0%, the paint layer would be invisible and of no use. Use a 600-pixel round soft airbrush on a flow of 40%. Sample a light

FIGURE 5-17

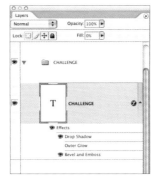

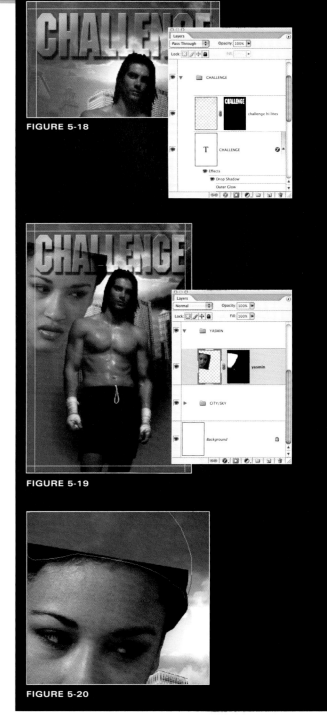

FIGURE 5-18

FIGURE 5-19

FIGURE 5-20

golden color from the sky and paint a few strokes at various places to define the type while maintaining its transparent quality (**FIGURE 5-18**). Save your document.

REPAIR THE TOP OF YASMIN'S HEAD AND BLEND HER INTO THE BACKGROUND

1. Show the group YASMIN. If necessary, lower the layer *yasmin* so the show title is in the middle of her forehead and not too close to her eyebrows. Rotate her slightly to the right, about 9.3 degrees, so her attention is directed toward the center of the poster.

2. Blend Yasmin's neck and shoulders into the background by adding a layer mask and painting with black and a large soft brush (about 150–200 pixels) on the layer mask. Be sure the hard edge of the original photo is concealed (**FIGURE 5-19**).

3. To repair the top of Yasmin's head, hide the groups CHAL-LENGE and TRES temporarily. Hide the guides. Add a new layer above *yasmin* and name it *top of head*. Use the Pen tool to make a path around what should be the top of her head. The lower portion of the path should be an arc that echoes her hairline (**FIGURE 5-20**). Load the path as a selection and add a 2-pixel feather. Use the eyedropper to sample the color of her hair and fill the selection with that color.

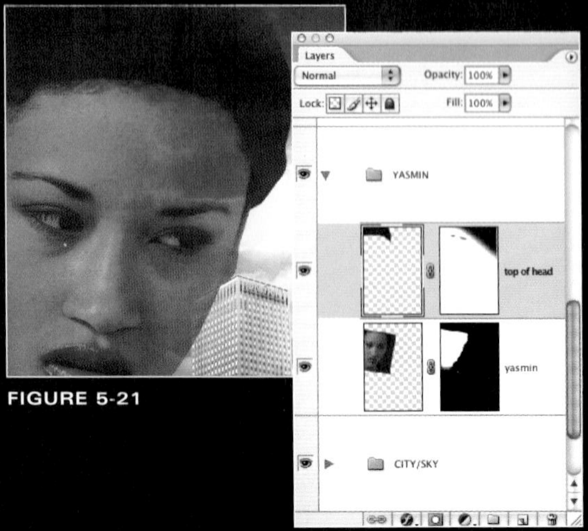

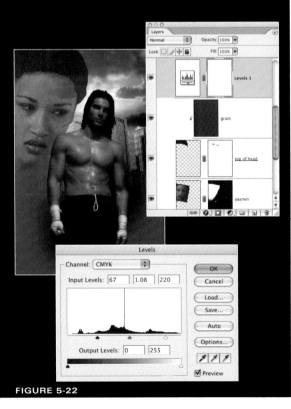

FIGURE 5-21

FIGURE 5-22

4. Deselect and add a layer mask to *top of head* and use the mask to soften the edge and blend the layer with her real hair. The fact that *yasmin* is cropped right at her hairline makes it difficult to create a believable hairline. However, the opacity of this group will be reduced and the show title will be over it. Both of these will distract attention and help make the hairline and top of the head credible. To help blend Yasmin into the background and disguise a less-than-perfect head repair, use a large soft airbrush on a flow of about 40% and, working on *top of head* layer mask, partially mask out the upper right side of the layer, causing it to fade or blend into the sky. Use a smaller brush and carefully paint over the joint between the actual top of Yasmin's head and the fake hair to blend them together and disguise the joint. It may help to hide the group TRES temporarily while doing this (**FIGURE 5-21**).

5. To make the paint layer less flat, add a grain overlay layer using the technique discussed in detail in **Mini-Tutorial 4**. Here's a brief review: With *top of head* highlighted, Option/Alt-click the *Create new layer* button at the bottom of the Layers palette. In the New Layer dialog, name the layer *grain*, choose Use Previous Layer to Create Clipping Mask, select Overlay from the Mode menu, then check Fill with Overlay-neutral color and click OK. Go to Filter > Noise > Add Noise. Add about 40% noise, choose Gaussian for Distribution, and click OK. Go to Filter > Blur > Gaussian and blur the noise about 0.4 pixels. Lower the opacity of the grain layer to about 30%.

6. Next add an adjustment layer to increase the contrast of the YASMIN group. To keep the adjustment layer from affecting all layers below, **change the blending mode for the group YASMIN from Pass Through to Normal**. Then add a Levels adjustment layer above the grain layer. Use the Levels to increase the contrast of the group (**FIGURE 5-22**). Lower the opacity of the **group** to 60%.

7. The clouds showing through Yasmin's face add a romantic, ethereal look, but the buildings showing through under the eye on the left are not attractive. Highlight the *city* layer and, working on the layer mask, conceal the buildings on the left under her eye. The building on the other side of her face, under her cheek, is less distracting and can remain. If the clouds are showing through too much try revealing more of the *Color Fill red* layer.

8. Show the layer *CHALLENGE* to see how everything works together so far (**FIGURE 5-23**). Save your document.

Posterized elements

The sidebar on "selling" your design explained the choices and meanings of these images. This portion of the project will address their treatment in Photoshop to get the desired effects in the poster.

Open **Fence.tif**, **Desert.tif**, and **Running.tif**. These elements will be treated in a very flat, graphic way as opposed to a realistic, photographic way (Running.tif has already been created that way). I refer to them as *posterized* because to me they resemble flat, silk-screened graphics. *Posterized* in Photoshop refers to a multicolored image in which the number of colors is reduced so gradations and transitions are eliminated—and there is a filter that will do just that. Here, we're using *posterize* a little differently. The technique I will show you doesn't use the Posterize filter and it reduces the image to a single, rather than multiple, color. The effect is much like an ink illustration. This flat monotone effect will contrast with the photographic elements and add an illustrative quality. (I felt a running image was important both to the story and for its symbolic aspects, but I couldn't find the right image in the stock photography library. This image is an illustration I created by referring to a variety of images. It will work in this situation because it is a silhouette. If I needed a photographic image I would need to find someone to model for me and shoot the image myself.)

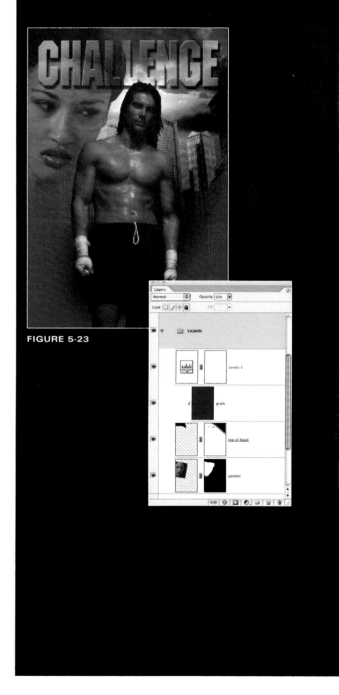

FIGURE 5-23

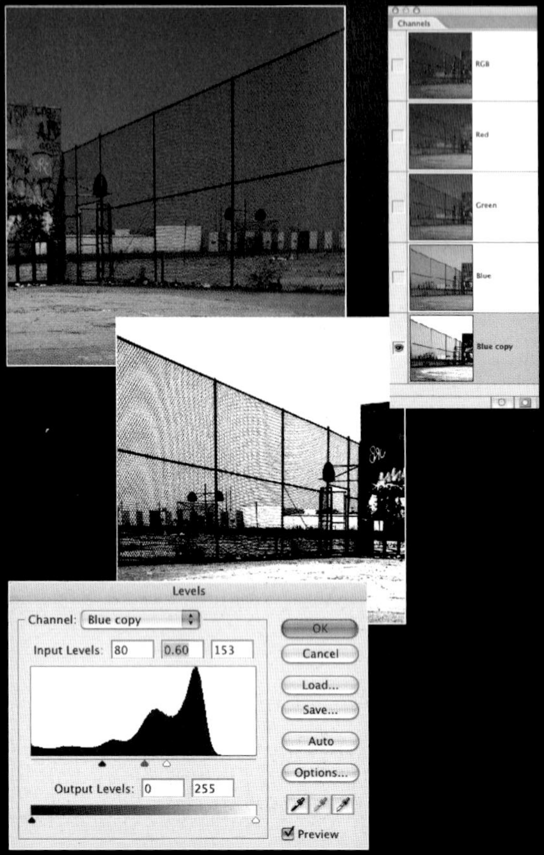

FIGURE 5-24

FIGURE 5-25

1. Make Fence.tif the active image. This photo will work better flipped with the angle of the fence leading the eye into the picture rather than out. In the main menu choose Image > Rotate Canvas > Flip Canvas Horizontal. Open the Channels palette and look at each channel to find the one with the most contrast. That is the blue channel. Duplicate that channel, creating an alpha channel. Use Image > Adjustments > Levels (Command-L/Ctrl-L) to increase the contrast by moving the highlights triangle (the one on the right) toward the left to force the whites toward black. Move the shadows triangle to the right, forcing the darks toward white and click OK. The channel should look like a black-and-white line illustration (**FIGURE 5-24**).

2. Load the *Blue copy* alpha channel as a selection (Command/Ctrl-click on the channel's thumbnail). Highlight the RGB composite channel and hide the alpha channel. Add a new layer in the Layers palette named *fence*. Notice which areas are selected. If the sky is selected, inverse the selection (Command-Shift-I/Ctrl-Shift-I). (Which area is selected is determined by the last choice made regarding "Color Indicates" when adding an alpha channel.) Fill the selection with black. Fill it again to get a more solid black (**FIGURE 5-25**). Save the file as Fence.psd.

3. Activate Desert.tif. You will be using only the rough, hilly terrain in the foreground. In the Channels palette, find the channel containing the most contrast in that area and duplicate it. Use Levels to increase the contrast (**FIGURE 5-26**).

4. Load that channel as a selection. If the dark area of the image is not selected, invert the selection. In the Layers palette, add a new layer named *desert* and fill the selection with very dark brown (**FIGURE 5-27**).

5. To select only the foreground area and mask out the rest, hide the original *Background* layer and add a layer above it. Fill the new layer with white. The purpose of this layer is simply to hide the checkerboard pattern so you can more easily see what's going on. Use the Pen tool and make a path around the foreground hills, load the path as a selection, add a 1-pixel feather and a layer mask (**FIGURE 5-28**).

FIGURE 5-26

FIGURE 5-27

FIGURE 5-28

COMPOSITE POSTERIZED ELEMENTS IN FINAL DOCUMENT

1. Make a new group in P5.psd named FENCE/DESERT above the group YASMIN. Drag *fence* from Fence.psd into the new group. Use Free Transform to scale *fence* up 160%. Carefully position the fence so the bars don't cross Yasmin's eyes or the middle of her mouth.

2. Add a layer mask and choose the Gradient tool. Make sure the foreground color is black and choose Foreground to Transparent preset. Mask the right side and bottom. A portion of the lower left of the image will be revealed again when you bring in *desert*. Use a large soft airbrush on a flow of about 10% to subtly reduce the opacity of the fence over Yasmin's face. Don't eliminate it completely, just make her face come through a bit. Change the blending mode to Multiply (**FIGURE 5-29**).

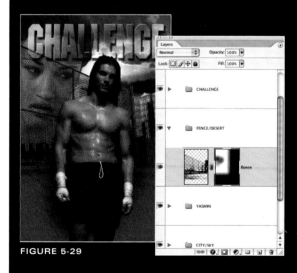

FIGURE 5-29

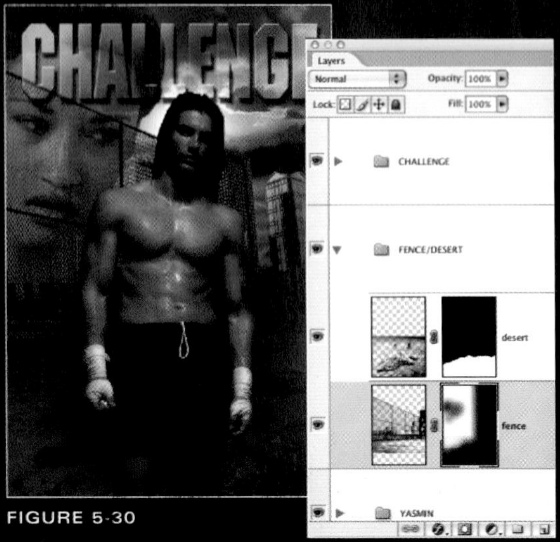

FIGURE 5-30

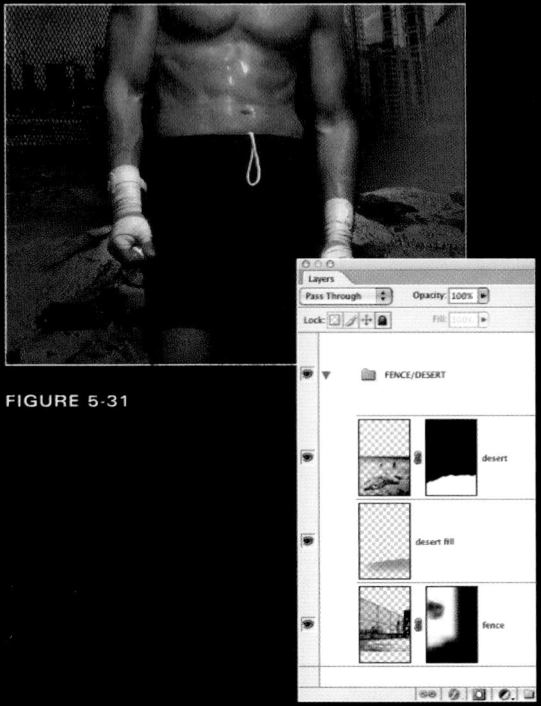

FIGURE 5-31

3. Drag the layer *desert* from Desert.tif into the FENCE/DESERT group in P5.psd. Position it so the bottom of *desert* is aligned with the bottom of the image. Now, paint with white on the layer mask to reveal the lower left portion of *fence* to fill the space between *desert* and *fence* (**FIGURE 5-30**).

4. To give *desert* definition and create a sense of light source, make a new layer below desert named *desert fill* and, with either the Lasso or Pen tool, make a selection in the shape of the desert area. Add a 3-pixel feather. Use a 600-pixel airbrush and sample a yellow-orange from the sky (similar to C=0, M=52, Y=95, K=0). With the airbrush flow at about 30%, paint highlights along the top of the hills. The idea is to make the hills appear to be illuminated by the sun. Change the blending mode to Color Dodge; this will help blend the new color with the background (**FIGURE 5-31**).

Tip: Even though this is a montage composite where the various elements are not intended to appear as though they exist in the same space and time, using a common light source is a good way to unify the composite.

5. Activate Running.tif. Drag the layer *running* into the group FENCE/DESERT in P5.psd just above *desert*. Scale it to 120% and position it so the figure is at the top of the hill. Rotate *running* slightly to the right to counter the angle of the buildings, creating tension and a more dynamic energy. To create a cast shadow, duplicate the layer, name the copy *shadow*, and use the Free Transform command to Flip Vertical. With Free Transform still active, move the figure down and align the feet of the copied version with the feet of the original runner. Then distort the copy, creating the appearance of a long cast shadow. Lower the Layer opacity of *shadow* to 73% and change the blending mode to Multiply (**FIGURE 5-32**).

6. To help the running figure stand out, add a glow beyond the hill. Make a new layer named *running glow red* above *fence* and below the *desert fill* layer. First set the foreground color to red and with the Gradient tool on Radial Gradient, Foreground to Transparent, make a glow on the far side of the runner. On another new layer, *running glow yellow*, create another glow, this time using yellow. Use the Move tool to position these layers for the best effect and add a layer mask to modify the yellow glow, making it narrower and concealing where it overlaps the hilltop. Avoid centering the yellow glow directly behind the runner—it will look more natural if it is off to the side. Change the blending mode on the yellow glow to Color Dodge and lower the opacity to 80% (**FIGURE 5-33**). Close Running.tif and Desert.tif.

Finishing touches

ADD DETAIL TO TRES' HAIR

Getting hair to look natural is really tough. If a strong contrast exists between the hair and the background, "pulling a channel mask" is the way to go. That is essentially what you did when you posterized the fence and desert. But this image has very little contrast between the hair and background, and channels will be of little use. During the initial masking stage when you separated Tres from the background, you defined the larger chunks and bumps of hair, but the hair still looked cut out and unnatural. To get a natural look, you'll now use a very small brush and work on the layer mask to reveal and conceal, not exactly individual hairs, but small groups of hairs. This isn't dry, fluffy hair, it's thick and wet with sweat. You want to capture that quality if you can. Details such as this add authenticity.

1. In this and following steps you will be using adjustment layers. To prevent these from affecting the layers below, change the blending mode for the group TRES to Normal.

2. Start by duplicating the layer *tres*. Hide the original layer. It is really the original layer mask you want to preserve. You will be working nondestructively, so the image itself is in no danger. But painting in hair can be very tricky and you may mess up the mask to the point that you want to start over.

3. To help separate the hair from the background, temporarily disable the layer mask by pressing Shift and clicking on the layer mask. Add a temporary Levels adjustment layer above it. Push

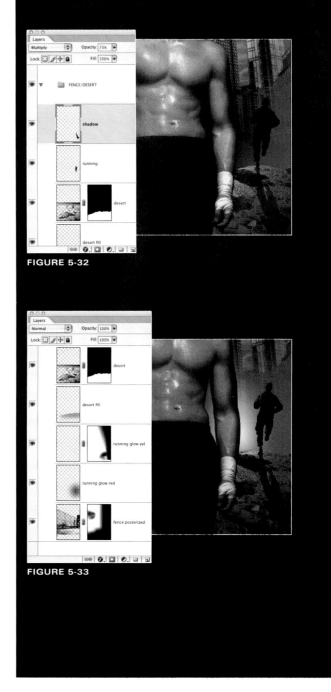

FIGURE 5-32

FIGURE 5-33

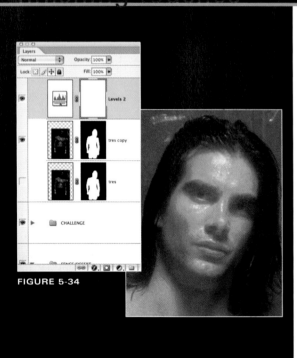

FIGURE 5-34

FIGURE 5-35

the middle slider to the left to open up the shadow areas so you can more easily differentiate the hair from the background. This will make his face look very weird, but, don't worry, this adjustment layer will be discarded shortly (**FIGURE 5-34**).

4. The hair should be fairly well separated from the background now. Use a small brush, about 10 pixels in diameter. Open the Brushes palette and turn on Shape Dynamics. Select Pen Pressure in the Size Jitter field if you are working with a stylus and graphics tablet. A tapering stroke will look more natural than one of consistent width that suddenly comes to an end. With Pen Pressure selected you can vary the width of the stroke by varying the pressure on the stylus, and instead of ending bluntly the strokes can taper to nice points. Although the layer mask for *tres copy* is currently disabled, you can still paint on it—but you won't see the results of your work until you enable the mask. As you paint, use swift, flowing strokes. Try to get a feel for the flow of the hair. Enable the mask from time to time (Shift-click on the mask) to see the results. If you don't like a stroke press X to switch from black to white and remove the stroke. Continue to toggle back and forth between black and white to fine-tune the mask. Shift-click on the mask to turn it on and off as you go, to see the results of your work. To see what the mask itself looks like, Option/Alt-click on the mask thumbnail in the Layers palette (**FIGURE 5-35**). When you are happy with the mask, discard the Levels adjustment layer. You can also discard the original *tres* layer. Rename *tres copy* as *tres*.

REMOVE THE DRAWSTRING AND FIX TRES' ARM

1. The white drawstring on Tres' shorts is distracting. To remove it, highlight *tres*. With the Lasso make a selection around a portion of the shorts and stomach just left of the drawstring. Add a 3-pixel feather and press Command-J/Ctrl-J. This copies and pastes the selection onto its own layer. Use the Move tool to position that piece over the drawstring. Rotate the layer slightly to line up the stitches in the waistband. Add a layer mask, then use a brush and paint with black on the layer mask to blend the layer with the image below (**FIGURE 5-36**).

2. Next, we need to fix the area on his arm where the other boxer's hand was. In the original image, the other boxer's hand and wrist are actually resting on Tres' arm. If you accurately masked Tres' arm, really paying attention to the anatomy, there should be a small portion of the other boxer's hand and wrist on Tres' upper arm. This area can easily be fixed by using a paint layer with a grain overlay.

➤ Add a layer above the previously created layer and name it *paint – arm*. Use a soft airbrush, sample the dark color on the edge of Tres' arm near the area you wish to repair. Paint over the area. Don't worry about the paint going beyond his arm; you will add a layer mask to confine it.

➤ Command/Ctrl-click on the *tres* layer mask to load that mask as a selection and add a layer mask to the *paint – arm* layer. Whenever you use a paint layer it is a good idea to add a grain (noise) overlay layer to match the texture of the surrounding area. Add the grain overlay layer and apply the noise. The noise will be much too small, so select the area around the painted area and scale the noise about 190%. Blur the noise 1 pixel and reduce the Layer opacity to 23% (**FIGURE 5-37**).

MAKE TRES' BLACKS BLACKER AND INCREASE HIGHLIGHTS

Black comes in many varieties. It can be a challenge to get all the blacks in a composite to match. That could be a tutorial all its own. In our composite it is obvious that the blacks in the image of Tres do not match the black in the fence, for example. To make the blacks in Tres blacker, you will use a Channel Mixer adjustment layer. Then, you will increase the overall contrast with a Levels adjustment layer. To add dimension to Tres' face you will add a Curves adjustment layer.

If you're unfamiliar with Channel Mixer or feel that a bit of brush-up would give you more confidence, take a break to read **Photoshop Essential 5**.

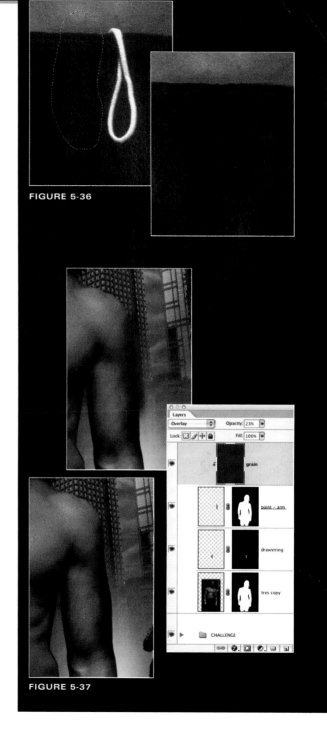

FIGURE 5-36

FIGURE 5-37

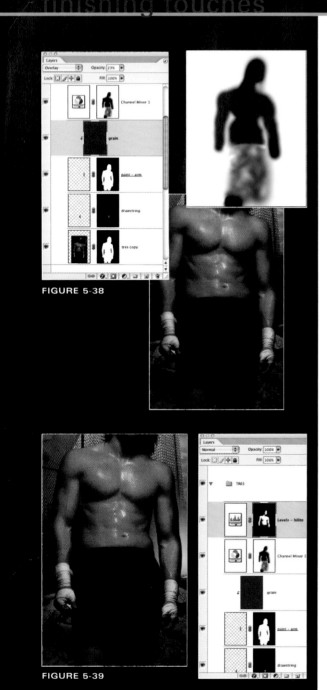

FIGURE 5-38

FIGURE 5-39

1. Add a Channel Mixer adjustment layer at the top of the stack in the group TRES. When working in CMYK, the Channel Mixer modifies the amount of ink that will be used to print the image. Adding other colors of ink to the black areas will produce a deeper, richer black. Select the black channel from the Output Channel menu and increase the cyan and magenta by +10, the yellow by +18; the black should be 100%. This gives you a much better black, but it also makes the midtones and high-lights darker. To restrict the adjustment to only the black areas, use the adjustment layer's mask to hide the areas you don't want to be affected. This will increase contrast and emphasize Tres' physique. Also, while we want the shorts darker, we don't want to lose the subtle highlights on the folds in the fabric of the shorts, because they add three-dimensionality. Those areas need to masked out as well (**FIGURE 5-38**).

2. Increase overall highlights on Tres with a Levels adjustment layer. First, add a new Levels adjustment layer above the Chan-nel Mixer layer. Move the highlight slider to the left to lighten Tres overall. Fill the adjustment layer mask with black to hide the effect of the adjustment layer. With a brush, use white to reveal the adjustment layer only in the areas you wish to lighten, avoiding the shadow areas (**FIGURE 5-39**).

3. To add highlights to Tres' face, add a Curves adjustment layer above the Levels layer. Add a point in the middle of the curve and drag it down slightly. This will lighten the entire image. Fill the layer mask with black and then use white to reveal the adjustment layer on his forehead, along his nose, on his cheek-bones, and on his chin. This adds more dimension to his face (**FIGURE 5-40**).

TINTS AND GLOWS

To make Tres stand out more, make the type easier to read, and pop the title we will use a series of paint layers I am calling tints and glows. These need to be in their own group because since group TRES is set to Normal blending mode, the blending modes will have no effect on layers outside the group. We will use three glow layers behind Tres to separate him from the background. These glows should be irregular, having an organic rather than a deliberate and predictable quality. That's why we are using paint layers rather than Outer Glow from layer styles. The three layers will be orange, yellow, and white with the darkest color lowest down in the stacking order.

1. Make a new group TINTS/GLOWS above FENCE/DESERT and add a new layer named *tres – orange glow*. Use a large soft airbrush, 20% flow with orange paint, and paint irregular strokes behind Tres. With the airbrush if you slow down or stop you put down more paint. This is desirable because it adds an irregular quality. Lower the Layer opacity and put the layer on Color Dodge blending mode. Use the layer mask to refine the painting (**FIGURE 5-41**).

2. Add two more layers, a yellow and a white layer. When painting with the yellow restrict the area more around the upper body; with the white layer restrict the paint to right around the head. This will draw attention to Tres' face. Leave both of these layers at 100% opacity. Leave the blending mode for the yellow layer on Normal, but change the blending mode for the white layer to Hard Light (**FIGURE 5-42**).

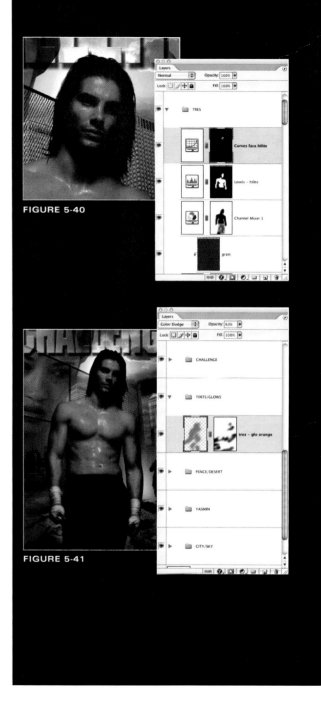

FIGURE 5-40

FIGURE 5-41

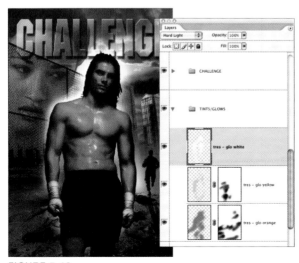

FIGURE 5-42

FINAL OUTPUT CONSIDERATIONS

The star's name and body copy you created in the this project are for comping purposes only. Unless a layer style or some other effect is being applied to the type, the final type is usually set in a vector-based page layout program. If all the type in the file was set in Photoshop and not rasterized (flattened), and there were no other placed images (such as vector-based logos), it would be possible to output the poster directly from Photoshop. However, that is usually not the case. Here are some reasons why.

Although I generally include the layered psd file when I send everything to the printer, a file of this size can take a long time to print. To speed printing I will save the file as a flattened tiff. That will automatically rasterize everything in the file, including the vector type. To get clean type, the tiff will have to be placed in a page layout application and the type reset. Be sure to run a spelling check when you set the final type.

Corporate logos are an important consideration in every ad or poster. Often companies team up to produce, finance or distribute a film. Many times they will share the cost of printing the poster or publishing the ad. They will require that they be given credit by way of having their logos clearly displayed. As the designer, you will want these logos as small as possible, but most logos are created in vector-based applications and when imported into Photoshop and reduced they really look bad. Whenever possible, these logos should be used as vector art and placed in a vector-based page layout program for final output. Or, take advantage of CS2's new Smart Objects feature. This allows you to

embed another image in your file but maintain the editability of the embedded image. This means you can link to a vector-based image (an Illustrator file, for example) without rasterizing it as you would by placing into Photoshop. The caveat is that you must either output the composite file to a PostScript device or as a pdf file.

The billing or credit block usually goes at the bottom of the poster. To accommodate the large quantity of information and legal requirements regarding the height of persons' names, this block of copy can grow quite complicated. The names will be set at the required height but descriptions, such as *Produced by,* are often stacked and set in a much smaller point size so as to take up less room. Changes should be expected in this copy after it goes to the producers and their attorneys for approval. For these reasons it is usually more practical to set this copy in another program.

All items being sent out for printing or publications should contain crop marks and legends. The legend should include information such as the job title, version (if there have been revisions), name of publication (if an ad), date of publication, the name of the company you are working for (or your own company name) and anything else pertinent to the job. I often include dimensions. This forces me to double-check my sizes and helps the printer/press house make sure everything is correct. While it is possible to include these in a Photoshop file, it is easier to do it in a page layout program.

Color is potentially a problem. Always get a color proof and, whenever possible, do a press check. A press check takes place at the printing press when the job is actually being printed. Obviously, you can't do a press check for an ad being printed in a magazine, but you can for a poster. At the press check, the press will be warmed up by printing a few hundred sheets. Then one of the sheets will be pulled for you, the printing company's rep, and the pressman to examine. It would be a good idea to have your client there as well, but since most press checks occur at odd hours, this may not be feasible. Most presses are computerized these days and subtle changes in the ink density and mixture can easily be made. When you are happy with the color, you will sign the sheet and go on your way. It is the pressman's responsibility to insure that all the rest of the prints match the one you approved. ■

3. Add another layer above *tres – glow white* named *dark frame*. With a large (200-pixel) soft airbrush on a flow of about 35%, use black to paint an irregular border around the entire image. Make a larger patch in the lower left to accommodate body copy. Add a layer mask and paint with black on the mask to finesse the shape. Do not completely cover the small amount of blue sky in the upper right. Even a small portion of a cool color will intensify the warmth of the other colors. Change the Layer blending mode to Multiply. Use the layer's opacity setting to control the effect (**FIGURE 5-43**).

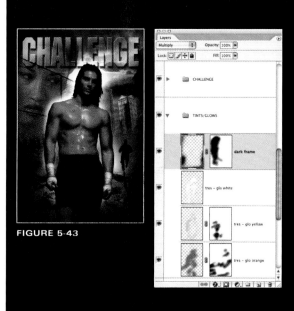

FIGURE 5-43

COMPLETE THE TITLE TREATMENT, STAR BILLING, AND BODY COPY

To finish up the title treatment you will add more paint layers to make the word *CHALLENGE* pop and create the *FINAL* portion of the title.

1. Begin by adding three more paint layers to the top of the CHALLENGE group. The purpose of these is to make the type more legible by adding contrast around the edges. You may find it easier to see the effect if you hide the edges of the selection (View > Extras; Command-H/Ctrl-H) Command/Ctrl-click on

FIGURE 5-44

FIGURE 5-45

the word CHALLENGE to load it as a selection. Use a large soft brush and yellow to paint over the type and thus define the bottom left and top central area of the title; change the blending mode to Color Dodge. On the next layer use blue to define the upper right edge, change the blending mode to Color Dodge. Use red on the next layer to define the upper left edge, and change the blending mode to Hard Light (**FIGURE 5-44**).

2. Choose the Type tool, make the color bright red, the point size 96.4, tracking 230, the font Helvetica Bold. Type *FINAL*. Helvetica Bold doesn't really have the weight needed to give this word presence. Helvetica Black is too heavy combined with the font used for CHALLENGE. To get something in between, duplicate the layer, rasterize the duplicate layer (Layer > Rasterize > Type) and, in the main menu go to Edit > Stroke and add a 2-point stroke in the same red color to the outside of the letters. FINAL should be centered vertically in the word CHALLENGE and appear centered horizontally. You will need to visually center the word horizontally; if it is truly centered it will appear slightly too far left because of the shape of the letter L (**FIGURE 5-45**).

3. Option/Alt-drag the Bevel and Emboss effect from CHALLENGE to FINAL, then open the Layer Style dialog and add an outer glow. Make the color white, the blending mode Color Dodge. Opacity 75, Spread 12, and Size 40 (**FIGURE 5-46**).

4. Make a new group above TRES named BODY COPY/BILLING. This will contain the star's name and body copy. The star's name, TRES MARIOS, has to go above the title. It can be right at live, but there needs to be a little breathing room between it and the word CHALLENGE. If necessary, select the groups TRES and CHALLENGE and move them down slightly. With the new group highlighted, choose the Type tool. Select Helvetica Bold (or something similar), color white, about 33.8 points, tracking set to 1000, and type *TRES MARIOS*. Center the type over CHALLENGE.

5. For the body copy use Helvetica Bold Condensed or some other sans serif condensed font. Make the size about 31.5 points, the leading about 61.5, and the tracking about –10. The exact amounts may varying depending upon the font you choose. From the Paragraph palette, choose *Left align text* (flush left). The body copy reads "A born loser with one chance to beat the odds." Stack and break the lines so the copy wraps around Tres' arm and hand (**FIGURE 5-47**).

FIGURE 5-46

FIGURE 5-47

A color channel represents in grayscale the distribution of tonal values for a particular color in your image. Modify the distribution of values for a color channel, and you change the way that color appears in the image. With the Channel Mixer adjustment layer you can do this nondestructively. This can be used for simple color corrections, to convert a color image to grayscale, or to radically change the color makeup of the image (**PE 5**).

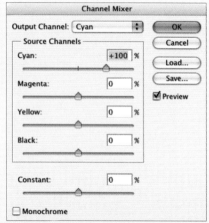

PE 5

At the top of the Channel Mixer dialog you can select which channel to modify—the output channel. In a CMYK image, there will be four channels to choose from. Each represents a color of ink that will be used to reproduce the job on press. In the the Source Channels pane are sliders that let you use data from the other channels to modify the currently selected output channel. Initially, the percentage for the color corresponding to the output channel is 100% and the other colors are 0%. So, for example, with the Cyan channel selected as the output channel, in the Source Channels pane Cyan will be at 100% and all of the other colors will be at 0%. By moving the sliders left or right you add or subtract grayscale information from other channels and change the distribution of cyan ink in the image.

In this project you will use Channel Mixer to make a four-color black. You may think that black is black is black, but actually there are many variations of black. A four-color black is much richer and darker than black composed of only 100% black ink. With a Channel Mixer adjustment layer you can modify the blacks on a single layer without affecting the blacks in the rest of the image.

Channel Mixer is also a great way to convert an image to grayscale. There are times when, for artistic effect, you want to have a grayscale image as part of a full-color or limited-color composite. In the Channel Mixer dialog, check the Monotone box at the bottom, then move the sliders to fine tune the brightness and contrast.

…and that's a wrap

The projects in this book have given you a solid foundation in the Photoshop skills you need to pursue a career in entertainment marketing. The special demands of entertainment marketing develop skills that apply anywhere. I hope you will take what you have learned and create amazing, compelling, and award-winning advertising.

The value of what you have learned is by no means restricted to print advertising. Whether you end up producing on-air graphics, DVD menus, video games, or websites, mastery of the tools and techniques discussed in this book will give you tremendous creative power, unlocking the doors to your imagination and to career opportunities. Photoshop has opened a whole new world to me. It has let me make a living doing something I truly enjoy.

You have learned a great deal in these pages, but there is always more to learn. Don't see that as a reason to be discouraged, but rather embrace it with enthusiasm and enjoy the process.

appendix

Selected keyboard shortcuts

Keyboard shortcuts will speed you along in everything you do with Photoshop. Here is a list of the most frequently used shortcuts—dozens of others can be found in Photoshop Help.

OPERATION	MAC SHORTCUT	WINDOWS SHORTCUT
Reset foreground to white and background to black (default)	D	D
Swap foreground and background colors	X	X
Undo	Command-Z	Ctrl-Z
Group (use previous layer as clipping mask)	Command-G	Ctrl-G
Ungroup	Command-Shift-G	Ctrl-Shift-G
Select all	Command-A	Ctrl-A
Hide or show marching ants	Command-H	Ctrl-H
Feather selection	Command-Option-D	Ctrl-Alt-D
Deselect	Command-D	Ctrl-D
Hide/show tools, option bar, and palettes	Tab	Tab
Hide/show palettes only	Shiftf-Tab	Shiftf-Tab
Display Brushes palette	F5	F5
Select Brush tool	B	B

OPERATION	MAC SHORTCUT	WINDOWS SHORTCUT
Choose Airbrush when in Brush tool	Shift-Option-P	Shift-Alt-P
Free Transform tool	Command-T	Ctrl-T
Escape a tool	Command-period (.)	Ctrl-period (.)
Copy and paste in place on new layer	Command-J	Ctrl-J
Zoom in	Command-plus (+)	Ctrl-plus (+)
Zoom out	Command-minus (-)	Ctrl-minus (-)
Magnify to custom zoom ratio	Command-Spacebar-drag	Ctrl-Spacebar-drag
Fit image to screen	Command-0 (zero)	Ctrl-0 (zero)
Scroll image with Hand tool	Spacebar-drag	Spacebar-drag
Curves	Command-M	Ctrl-M
Levels	Command-L	Ctrl-L
Hue and Saturation	Command-U	Ctrl-U
Show or conceal guides	Command-semicolon (;)	Ctrl-semicolon (;)
Show or hide rulers	Command-R	Ctrl-R

Tools and techniques covered in this book

You may wish to go back and review a specific tool or technique from time to time. Rather than leaf through the book to find it, here's a useful cross-reference.

WHAT WAS IN EACH PROJECT?

PROJECT 1	PROJECT 2	PROJECT 3	PROJECT 4	PROJECT 5
Airbrush	Adjustment Layers	Alpha channels	Body parts, mix & match	Channel Mixer
Blur filter	Free Transform	Color Picker	Clone Stamp tool	Layer fill
Color Picker	Lasso tool	Colorize	Color correction	Posterizing
Gradient tool	Layer masks	Curves	Healing Brush	Rescaling (Enlarging)
Gradient Editor	Layers, Adjustment	Layer Styles	Mix & match body parts	
Layer Blend Modes	Marquee tool	Levels	Retouching using a paint layer with a grain overlay	
Layer Clipping Masks	Paths	Type tool	Shape Layers	
Magic Wand tool	Pen tool and Paths		Shape tools	
Layers and Layer Groups	Selection tools; Marquee and Lasso		Spot Healing Brush	
	Transform		Vector masks	

WHICH PROJECT COVERED THIS?

TOOL OR TECHNIQUE	PROJECT
Adjustment layers	2
Airbrush	1
Alpha Channels	3
Blur filter	1
Channel Mixer	5
Clone Stamp tool	4
Color correction	4
Color Picker	1
Colorize	3
Curves	3
Free Transform	2
Gradient tool and Gradient Editor	1
Healing Brush	4
Lasso tool	2
Layers and Layer Groups	1
Layer Blend Modes	1
Layer Clipping Masks	1
Layer Fill	5
Layer Masks	2

TOOL OR TECHNIQUE	PROJECT
Layer styles	3
Layers, adjustment	2
Levels	3
Magic Wand tool	1
Marquee tool	2
Mix and match body parts	4
Paths	2
Pen tool and Paths	2
Posterizing	5
Resampling (enlarging)	5
Retouching using a paint layer with a grain overlay	4
Selection tools; Marquee and Lasso	2
Shape Layers	4
Shape tools	4
Spot Healing Brush	4
Transform	2
Type tool	3
Vector Masks	4

index

B

C

Image # 1610031

Image # Plo42004

Image # 1540029

Image # Plo55017